Three Years in Europe
Places I Have Seen and People I Have Met

William Wells Brown

Contents

PREFACE.	23
LETTER I.	24
LETTER II.	29
LETTER III.	36
LETTER IV.	45
LETTER V.	51
LETTER VI.	57
LETTER VII.	65
LETTER VIII.	70
LETTER IX.	82
LETTER X.	88
LETTER XI.	97
LETTER XII.	103
LETTER XXIII.	113
LETTER XIII.	117
LETTER XIV.	125
LETTER XV.	129
LETTER XVI.	136
LETTER XVII.	142
LETTER XVIII.	148
LETTER XIX.	152
LETTER XX.	157
LETTER XXI.	165
LETTER XXII.	177

THREE YEARS IN EUROPE

PLACES I HAVE SEEN AND PEOPLE I HAVE MET

BY

William Wells Brown

MEMOIR OF WILLIAM WELLS BROWN.

A narrative of the life of the author of the present work has been most extensively circulated in England and America. The present memoir will, therefore, simply comprise a brief sketch of the most interesting portion of Mr. Brown's history while in America, together with a short account of his subsequent cisatlantic career. The publication of his adventures as a slave, and as a fugitive from slavery in his native land, has been most valuable in sustaining a sound anti-slavery spirit in Great Britain. His honourable reception in Europe may be equally serviceable in America, as another added to the many practical protests previously entered from this side of the Atlantic, against the absolute bondage of three millions and a quarter of the human race, and the semi-slavery involved in the social and political proscription of 600,000 free coloured people in that country.

William Wells Brown was born at Lexington, in the state of Kentucky, as nearly as he can tell in the autumn of 1814. In the Southern States of America, the pedigree and age of a horse or a dog are carefully preserved, but no record is kept of the birth of a slave. All that Mr. Brown knows upon the subject is traditionally, that he was born "about corn-cutting time" of that year. His mother was a slave named Elizabeth, the property of Dr. Young, a physician. His father was George Higgins, a relative of his master.

The name given to our author at his birth, was "William"--no second or surname being permitted to a slave. While William was an infant, Dr. Young removed to Missouri, where, in addition to his profession as a physician, he carried on the--to European notions--incongruous avocations of miller, merchant, and farmer. Here William was employed as a house servant, while his mother was engaged as a field hand. One of his first bitter experiences of the cruelties of slavery, was his witnessing the infliction of ten lashes upon the bare back of his mother, for being a few minutes behind her time at the field--a punishment inflicted with one of those peculiar whips in the construction of which, so as to produce the greatest amount of torture, those whom Lord Carlisle has designated "the chivalry of the South" find scope for their ingenuity.

Dr. Young subsequently removed to a farm near St. Louis, in the same State. Having been elected a Member of the Legislature, he devolved the management of his farm upon an overseer, having, what to his unhappy victims must have been the ironical name of "Friend Haskall." The mother and child were now separated. The boy was levied to a Virginian named Freeland, who bore the military title of Major, and carried on the plebeian business of a publican. This man was of an extremely brutal disposition, and treated his slaves with most refined cruelty. His favourite punishment, which he facetiously called "Virginian play," was to flog his slaves severely, and then expose their lacerated flesh to the smoke of tobacco stems, causing the most exquisite agony. William complained to his owner of the treatment of Freeland, but, as in almost all similar instances, the appeal was in vain. At length he was induced to attempt an escape, not from that love of liberty which subsequently became with him an unconquerable passion, but simply to avoid the cruelty to which he was habitually subjected. He took refuge in the woods, but was hunted and "traced" by the blood-hounds of a Major O'Fallon, another of "the chivalry of the South," whose gallant occupation was that of keeping an establishment for the hire of ferocious dogs with which to hunt fugitive slaves. The young slave received a severe application of "Virginia play" for his attempt to escape. Happily the military publican soon afterwards failed in business, and William found a better master and a more congenial employment with Captain Cilvers, on board a steam-boat plying between St. Louis and Galena. At the close of the sailing season he was levied to an hotel-keeper, a native of a free state, but withal of a class which exist north as well as south--a most inveterate negro hater. At this period of William's history, a circumstance occurred, which, although a common incident in the lives of slaves, is one of the keenest trials they have to endure--the breaking up of his family circle. Her master wanted money, and he therefore sold Elizabeth and six of her children to seven different purchasers. The family relationship is almost the only solace of slavery. While the mother, brothers, and sisters are permitted to meet together in the negro hut after the hour of labour, the slaves are comparatively content with their oppressed condition; but deprive them of this, the only privilege which they as human beings are possessed of, and nothing is left but the animal part of their nature--the living soul is extinguished within them. With them there is nothing to love--everything to hate. They feel themselves degraded to the condition not only of mere animals, but of the most ill-used animals in the creation.

Not needing the services of his young relative, Dr. Young hired him to the proprietor of the *St. Louis Times*, the best master William ever had in slavery. Here he gained the scanty amount of education he acquired at the South. This kind treatment by his editorial master appears to have engendered in the heart of William a consciousness of his own manhood, and led him into the commission of an offence similar to that perpetrated by Frederick Douglass, under similar circumstances--the assertion of the right of self-defence. He gallantly defended himself against the attacks of several boys older and bigger than himself, but in so doing was guilty of the unpardonable sin of lifting his hand against white lads; and the father of one of them, therefore, deemed it consistent with his manhood to lay in wait for the young slave, and beat him over the head with a heavy cane till the blood gushed from his nose and ears. From the effects of that treatment the poor lad was confined to his bed for five weeks, at the end of which time he found that, to his personal sufferings, were superadded the calamity of the loss of the best master he ever had in slavery.

His next employment was that of waiter on board a steam-boat plying on the Mississippi. Here his occupation again was pleasant, and his treatment good; but the freedom of action enjoyed by the passengers in travelling whithersoever they pleased, contrasted strongly in his mind with his own deprivation of will as a slave. The natural result of this comparison was an intense desire for freedom--a feeling which was never afterwards eradicated from his breast. This love of liberty was, however, so strongly counteracted by affection for his mother and sisters, that although urgently entreated by one of the latter to take advantage of his present favourable opportunity for escape, he would not bring himself to do so at the expense of a separation for life from his beloved relatives.

His period of living on board the steamer having expired, he was again remitted to field labour, under a burning sun. From that labour, from which he suffered severely, he was soon removed to the lighter and more agreeable occupation of house-waiter to his master. About this time Dr. Young, in the conventional phraseology of the locality, "got religion." The fruit of his alleged spiritual gain, was the loss of many material comforts to the slaves. Destitute of the resources of education, they were in the habit of employing their otherwise unoccupied minds on the Sunday in fishing and other harmless pursuits; these were now all put an end to. The Sabbath became a season of dread to William: he was required to drive the family to and from the church, a distance of four miles either way; and while they attended to the salvation of their souls within the building, he was compelled to attend to the horses without it, standing by them during divine service under a burning sun, or drizzling rain. Although William did not get the religion of his master, he acquired a family passion which appears to have been strongly intermixed with the devotional exercises of the household of Dr. Young--a love of sweet julep. In the evening, the slaves were required to attend family worship. Before commencing the service, it was the custom to hand a pitcher of the favourite beverage to every member of the family, not excepting the nephew, a child of between four and five years old. William was in the habit of watching his opportunity during the prayer and helping himself from the pitcher, but one day letting it fall, his propensity for this intoxicating drink was discovered, and he was severely punished for its indulgence.

In 1830, being then about sixteen years of age, William was hired to a slave-dealer named Walker. This change of employment led the youth away south and frustrated, for a time, his plans for escape. His experience while in this capacity furnishes some interesting, though painful, details of the legalized traffic in human beings carried on in the United States. The desperation to which the slaves are driven at their forced separation from husband, wife, children, and kindred, he found to be a frequent cause of suicide. Slave-dealers he discovered were as great adepts at deception in the sale of their commodity as the most knowing down-easter, or tricky horse dealer. William's occupation on board the steamer, as they steamed south, was to prepare the stock for the market, by shaving off whiskers and blacking the grey hairs with a colouring composition.

At the expiration of the period of his hiring with Walker, William returned to his master rejoiced to have escaped an employment so repugnant to his feelings. But this joy was not of long duration. One of his sisters who, although sold to another master had been living in the same city with himself and mother, was again sold to be sent away south, never in all probability to meet her sorrowing relatives. Dr. Young also, wanting money, intimated to his young kinsman that he was about to sell him. This intimation determined William, in conjunction with his mother, to attempt their escape. For ten nights they travelled northwards, hiding themselves in the woods by day. The mother and son at length deemed themselves safe from re-capture, and, although weary and foot-sore, were laying down sanguine plans for the acquisition of a farm in Canada, the purchase of the freedom of the six other members of the family still in slavery, and rejoicing in the anticipated happiness of their free home in Canada. At that moment three men made up to and seized them, bound the son and led him, with his desponding mother, back to slavery. Elizabeth was sold and sent away south, while her son became the property of a merchant tailor named Willi. Mr. Brown's description of the final interview between himself and his mother, is one of the most touching portions of his narrative. The mother, after expressing her conviction of the speedy escape from slavery by the hand of death, enjoined her child to persevere in his endeavours to gain his freedom by flight. Her blessing was interrupted by the kick and curse bestowed by her dehumanized master upon her beloved son.

After having been hired for a short time to the captain of the steam-boat ***Otto***, William was finally sold to Captain Enoch Price for 650 dollars. That the quickness and intelligence of William rendered him very valuable as a slave, is favoured by the evidence of Enoch Price himself, who states that he was offered 2000 dollars for Sanford (as he was called), in New Orleans. William was strongly urged by his new mistress to marry. To facilitate this object, she even went so far as to purchase a girl for whom she fancied he had an affection. He himself, however, had secretly resolved never to enter into such a connexion while in slavery, knowing that marriage, in the true and honourable sense of the term, could not exist among slaves. Notwithstanding the multitude of petty offences for which a slave is severely punished, it is singular that one crime--bigamy--is visited upon a white with severity, while no slave has ever yet been tried for it. In fact, the man is allowed to form connections with as many women, and the women with as many men, as they please.

At St. Louis, William was employed as coachman to Mr. Price; but when that gentleman subsequently took his family up the river to Cincinnati, Sanford acted as appointed steward. While lying off this city, the long-looked-for opportunity of escape presented itself; and on the 1st of January, 1834--he being then almost twenty years of age--succeeded in getting from the steamer to the wharf, and thence to the woods, where he lay concealed until the shades of night had set in, when he again commenced his journey northwards. While with Dr. Young, a nephew of that gentleman, whose christian name was William, came into the family: the slave was, therefore, denuded of the name of William, and thenceforth called Sanford. This deprivation of his original name he had ever regarded as an indignity, and having now gained his freedom he resumed his original name; and as there was no one by whom he could be addressed by it, he exultingly enjoyed the first-fruits of his freedom by calling himself aloud by his old name "William!" After passing through a variety of painful vicissitudes, on the eighth day he found himself destitute of pecuniary means, and unable, from severe illness, to pursue his journey. In that condition he was discovered by a venerable member of the Society of Friends, who placed him in a covered waggon and took him to his own house. There he remained about fifteen days, and by the kind treatment of his host and hostess, who were what in America are called "Thompsonians," he was restored to health, and supplied with the means of pursuing his journey. The name of this, his first kind benefactor, was "Wells Brown." As William had risen from the degradation of a slave to the dignity of a man, it was expedient that he should follow the customs of other men, and adopt a second name. His venerable friend, therefore, bestowed upon him his own name, which, prefixed by his former designation, made him "William Wells Brown," a name that will live in history, while those of the men who claimed him as property would, were it not for his deeds, have been unknown beyond the town in which they lived. In nine days from the time he left Wells Brown's house, he arrived at Cleveland, in the State of Ohio, where he found he could remain comparatively safe from the pursuit of the man-stealer. Having obtained employment as a waiter, he remained in that city until the following spring, when he procured an engagement on board a steam-boat plying on Lake Erie. In that situation he was enabled, during seven months, to assist no less than sixty-nine slaves to escape to Canada. While a slave he had regarded the whites as the natural enemies of his race. It was, therefore, with no small pleasure that he discovered the existence of the salt of America, in the despised Abolitionists of the Northern States. He read with assiduity the writings of Benjamin Lundy, William Lloyd Garrison, and others; and after his own twenty years' experience of slavery, it is not surprising that he should have enthusiastically embraced the principles of "total and immediate emancipation," and "no union with slaveholders."

In proportion as his mind expanded under the more favourable circumstances in which he was placed, he became anxious, not merely for the redemption of his race from personal slavery, but for the moral elevation of those among them who were free. Finding that habits of intoxication were too prevalent amongst his coloured brethren, he, in conjunction with others, commenced a temperance reformation in their body. Such was the success of their efforts that in three years, in the city of Buffalo alone, a society of upwards of 500 members was raised out of a coloured population of 700. Of that society Mr. Brown was thrice elected President.

The intellectual powers of our author, coupled with his intimate acquaintance with the workings of the slave system, recommended him to the Abolitionists as a man eminently qualified to arouse the attention of the people of the Northern States to the great national sin of America. In 1843 he was engaged as a lecturer by the Western New-York Anti-Slavery Society. From 1844 to 1847 he laboured in the anti-slavery cause in connection with the American Anti-Slavery Society, and from that period up to the time of his departure for Europe, in 1849, he was an agent of the Massachusetts Anti-Slavery Society. The records of those societies furnish abundant evidence of the success of his labours. From the Massachusetts Anti-Slavery Society he early received the following testimony:--

"Since Mr. Brown became an agent of the Massachusetts Anti-Slavery Society, he has lectured in very many of the towns of this Commonwealth, and won for himself general respect and approbation. He combines true self-respect with true humility, and rare judiciousness with great moral courage. Himself a fugitive slave, he can experimentally describe the situation of those in bonds as bound with them; and he powerfully illustrates the diabolism of that system which keeps in chains and darkness a host of minds, which, if free and enlightened, would shine among men like stars in a firmament."

Another member of that Society speaks thus of him:--"I need not attempt any description of the ability and efficiency which characterized his speaking throughout the meetings. To you who know him so well, it is enough to say that his lectures were worthy of himself. He has left an impression on the minds of the people, that few could have done. Cold, indeed, must be the heart that could resist the appeals of so noble a specimen of humanity, in behalf of a crushed and despised race."

Notwithstanding the celebrity Mr. Brown had acquired in the north, as a man of genius and talent, and the general respect his high character had gained him, the slave spirit of America denied him the rights of a citizen. By the constitution of the United States, he was every moment liable to be seized and sent back to slavery. He was in daily peril of a gradual legalized murder, under a system one of whose established economical principles is, that it is more profitable to work up a slave on a plantation in a short time, by excessive labour and cheap food, than to obtain a lengthened remuneration by moderate work and humane treatment. His only protection from such a fate was the anomaly of the ascendancy of the public opinion over the law of the country. So uncertain, however, was that tenure of liberty, that even before the passage of the Fugitive Slave Law, it was deemed expedient to secure the services of Frederick Douglass to the anti-slavery cause by the purchase of his freedom. The same course might have been taken to secure the labours of Mr. Brown, had he not entertained an unconquerable repugnance to its adoption. On the 10th of January, 1848, Enoch Price wrote to Mr. Edmund Quincy offering to sell Mr. Brown to himself or friends for 325 dollars. To this communication the fugitive returned the following pithy and noble reply:--

"I cannot accept of Mr. Price's offer to become a purchaser of my body and soul. God made me as free as he did Enoch Price, and Mr. Price shall never receive a dollar from me or my friends with my consent."

There were, however, other reasons besides his personal safety which led to Mr. Brown's visit to Europe. It was thought desirable always to have in England some talented man of colour who should be a living lie to the doctrine of the inferiority of the African race: and it was moreover felt that none could so powerfully advocate the cause of "those in bonds" as one who had actually been "bound with them." This had been proved in the extraordinary effect produced in Great Britain by Frederick Douglass in 1845 and 1846. The American Committee in connection with the Peace Congress were also desirous of sending to Europe coloured representatives of their Society, and Mr. Brown was selected for that purpose, and duly accredited by them to the Paris Congress.

On the 18th of July, 1849, a large meeting of the coloured citizens of Boston was held in Washington Hall to bid him farewell. At that meeting the following resolutions were unanimously adopted:--

"***Resolved***,--That we bid our brother, William Wells Brown, God speed in his mission to Europe, and commend him to the hospitality and encouragement of all true friends of humanity.

"***Resolved***,--That we forward by him our renewed protest against the American Colonization Society; and invoke for him a candid hearing before the British public, in reply to the efforts put forth there by the Rev. Mr. Miller, or any other agent of said Society."

Two days afterwards he sailed for Europe, encountering on his voyage his last experience of American prejudice against colour.

On the 28th of August he landed at Liverpool, a time and place memorable in his life as the first upon which he could truly call himself a free man upon God's earth. In the history of nations, as of individuals, there is often singular retributive mercy as well as retributive justice. In the seventeenth century the victims of monarchical tyranny in Great Britain found social and political freedom when they set foot upon Plymouth Rock in New England: in the nineteenth century the victims of the oppressions of the American Republic find freedom and social equality upon the shores of monarchical England. Liverpool, which seventy years back was so steeped in the guilt of negro slavery that Paine expressed his surprise that God did not sweep it from the face of the earth, is now to the hunted negro the Plymouth Rock of Old England. From Liverpool he proceeded to Dublin where he was warmly received by Mr. Haughton, Mr. Webb, and other friends of the slave, and publicly welcomed at a large meeting presided over by the first named gentleman.

The reception of Mr. Brown at the Peace Congress in Paris was most flattering. In a company, comprising a large portion of the ***elite*** of Europe, he admirably maintained his reputation as a public speaker. His brief address, upon that "war spirit of America which holds in bondage three million of his brethren," produced a profound sensation. At its conclusion the speaker was warmly greeted by Victor Hugo, the Abbe Duguerry, Emile de Girardin, the Pastor Coquerel, Richard Cobden, and every man of note in the Assembly. At the soiree given by M. De Tocqueville, the Minister for Foreign Affairs, and the other fetes given to the Members of the Congress, Mr. Brown was received with marked attention.

Having finished his Peace mission in France, he commenced an Anti-slavery tour in England and Scotland. With that independence of feeling which those who are acquainted with him know to be his chief characteristic, he rejected the idea of anything like eleemosynary support. He determined to maintain himself and family by his own exertions--by his literary labours, and the honourable profession of a public lecturer. His first metropolitan reception in England was at a large, influential, and enthusiastic meeting in the Music Hall, Stone Street. The members of the Whittington Club--an institution numbering nearly 2000 members, among whom are Lords Brougham, Dudley Coutts Stuart, and Beaumont; Charles Dickens, Douglass Jerrold, Martin Thackeray, Charles Lushington, M.P., Monckton Milnes, M.P., and several other of the most distinguished legislators and literary men and women in this country--elected Mr. Brown an honorary member of the Club, as a mark of respect to his character; and, as the following extract from the Secretary, Mr. Stundwicke, will show, as a protest against the distinctions made between man and man on account of colour in America:--"I have much pleasure in conveying to you the best thanks of the managing committee of this institution for the excellent lecture you gave here last evening on the subject of 'Slavery in America,' and also in presenting you in their names with an honorary membership of the Club. It is hoped that you will often avail yourself of its privileges by coming amongst us. You will then see, by the cordial welcome of the members, that they protest against the odious distinctions made between man and man, and the abominable traffic of which you have been the victim."

For the last three years Mr. Brown has been engaged in visiting and holding meetings in nearly all the large towns in the kingdom upon the question of American Slavery, Temperance, and other subjects. Perhaps no coloured individual, not excepting that extraordinary man, Frederick Douglass, has done more good in disseminating anti-slavery principles in England, Scotland, and Ireland.

In the spring of 1851, two most interesting fugitives, William and Ellen Craft, arrived in England. They had made their escape from the South, the wife disguised in male attire, and the husband in the capacity of her slave. William Craft was doing a thriving business in Boston, but in 1851 was driven with his wife from that city by the operation of the Fugitive Slave Law. For several months they travelled in company with Mr. Brown in this country, deepening the disgust created by Mr. Brown's eloquent denunciation of slavery by their simple but touching narrative. At length they were enabled to gratify their thirst for education by gaining admission to Lady Byron's school at Oakham, Surrey. In the month of May, Mr. Brown and Mr. and Mrs. Craft were taken by a party of anti-slavery friends to the Great Exhibition. The honourable manner in which they were received by distinguished persons to whom their history was known, and the freedom with which they perambulated the American department, was a salutary rebuke to the numerous Americans present, in regard to the great sin of their country--slavery; and its great folly--prejudice of colour. A curious circumstance occurred during the Exhibition. Among the hosts of American visitors to this country was Mr. Brown's late master, Enoch Price, who made diligent inquiry after his lost piece of property--not, of course, with any view to its reclamation--but, to the mutual regret of both parties, without success. It is gratifying to state that the master spoke highly of, and expressed a wish for the future prosperity of, his fugitive slave; a fact which tends to prove that prejudice of colour is to a very great extent a thing of locality and association. Had Mr. Price, however, left behind him letters of manumission for Mr. Brown, enabling him, if he chose, to return to his native land, he would have given a more practical proof of respect, and of the sincerity of his desire for the welfare of Mr. Brown.

It would extend these pages far beyond their proposed length were anything like a detailed account of Mr. Brown's anti-slavery labours in this country to be attempted. Suffice it to say that they have everywhere been attended with benefit and approbation. At Bolton an admirable address from the ladies was presented to him, and at other places he has received most honourable testimonials.

Since Mr. Brown left America, the condition of the fugitive slaves in his own country has, through the operation of the Fugitive Slave Law, been rendered so perilous as to preclude the possibility of return without the almost certain loss of liberty. His expatriation has, however, been a gain to the cause of humanity in this country, where an intelligent representative of the oppressed coloured Americans is constantly needed, not only to describe, in language of fervid eloquence, the wrongs inflicted upon his race in the United States, but to prevent their bonds being strengthened in this country by holding fellowship with slave-holding and slave-abetting ministers from America. In his lectures he has clearly demonstrated the fact, that the sole support of the slavery of the United States is its churches. This knowledge of the standing of American ministers in reference to slavery has, in the case of Dr. Dyer, and in many other instances, been most serviceable, preventing their reception into communion with British churches. Last year Mr. Brown succeeded in getting over to this country his daughters, two interesting girls twelve and sixteen years of age respectively, who are now receiving an education which will qualify them hereafter to become teachers in their turn--a description of education which would have been denied them in their native land. In 1834 Mr.

Brown married a free coloured woman, who died in January of the present year.

The condition of escaped slaves has engaged much of his attention while in this country. He found that in England no anti-slavery organization existed whose object was to aid fugitive slaves in obtaining an honourable subsistence in the land of their exile. In most cases they are thrown upon the support of a few warm-hearted anti-slavery advocates in this country, pre-eminent among whom stands Mr. Brown's earliest friend, Mr. George Thompson, M.P., whose house is rarely free from one or more of those who have acquired the designation of his "American constituents." This want has recently been attempted to be supplied, partly through Mr. Brown's exertions, and partly by the establishment of the Anglo-American Anti-Slavery Association.

On the 1st of August, 1851, a meeting of the most novel character was held at the Hall of Commerce, London, being a soiree given by fugitive slaves in this country to Mr. George Thompson, on his return from his American mission on behalf of their race. That meeting was most ably presided over by Mr. Brown, and the speeches made upon the occasion by fugitive slaves were of the most interesting and creditable description. Although a residence in Canada is infinitely preferable to slavery in America, yet the climate of that country is uncongenial to the constitutions of the fugitive slaves, and their lack of education is an almost insuperable barrier to their social progress. The latter evil Mr. Brown attempted to remedy by the establishment of a Manual Labour School in Canada.

A public meeting, attended by between 3000 and 4000 persons, was convened by Mr. Brown, on the 6th of January, 1851, in the City Hall, Glasgow, presided over by Mr. Hastie, one of the representatives of that city, at which meeting a resolution was unanimously passed approving of Mr. Brown's scheme, which scheme, however, never received that amount of support which would have enabled him to bring it into practice; and the plan at present only remains as an evidence of its author's ingenuity and desire for the elevation of his depressed race. Mr. Brown subsequently made, through the columns of the *Times* newspaper, a proposition for the emigration of American fugitive slaves, under fair and honourable terms, to the West Indies, where there is a great lack of that tillage labour which they are so capable of undertaking. This proposition has hitherto met with no better fate than its predecessor.

Mr. Brown's literary abilities may be partly judged of from the following pages. The amount of knowledge and education he has acquired under circumstances of no ordinary difficulty, is a striking proof of what can be done by combined genius and industry. His proficiency as a linguist, without the aid of a master, is considerable. His present work is a valuable addition to the stock of English literature. The honour which has hitherto been paid, and which, so long as he resides upon British soil, will no doubt continue to be paid to his character and talents, must have its influence in abating the senseless prejudice of colour in America, and hastening the time when the object of his mission, the abolition of the slavery of his native country, shall be accomplished, and that young Republic renouncing with penitence its national sin, shall take its proper place amongst the most free, civilized, and Christian nations of the earth.

    W.F.

PREFACE.

While I feel conscious that most of the contents of these Letters will be interesting chiefly to American readers, yet I may indulge the hope, that the fact of their being the first production of a Fugitive Slave, as a history of travels, may carry with them novelty enough to secure for them, to some extent, the attention of the reading public of Great Britain. Most of the letters were written for the private perusal of a few personal friends in America; some were contributed to "Frederick Douglass's paper," a journal published in the United States. In a printed circular sent some weeks since to some of my friends, asking subscriptions to this volume, I stated the reasons for its publication: these need not be repeated here. To those who so promptly and kindly responded to that appeal, I tender my most sincere thanks. It is with no little diffidence that I lay these letters before the public; for I am not blind to the fact, that they must contain many errors; and to those who shall find fault with them on that account, it may not be too much for me to ask them kindly to remember, that the author was a slave in one of the Southern States of America, until he had attained the age of twenty years; and that the education he has acquired, was by his own exertions, he never having had a day's schooling in his life.

    W. WELLS BROWN.

22, CECIL STREET, STRAND,
    LONDON.

LETTER I.

Departure from Boston--the Passengers--Halifax--the Passage--First Sight of Land--Liverpool.

LIVERPOOL, *July 28*.

On the 18th July, 1849, I took passage in the steam-ship *Canada*, Captain Judkins, bound for Liverpool. The day was a warm one; so much so, that many persons on board, as well as several on shore, stood with their umbrellas up, so intense was the heat of the sun. The ringing of the ship's bell was a signal for us to shake hands with our friends, which we did, and then stepped on the deck of the noble craft. The *Canada* quitted her moorings at half-past twelve, and we were soon in motion. As we were passing out of Boston Bay, I took my stand on the quarter-deck, to take a last farewell (at least for a time), of my native land. A visit to the old world, up to that time had seemed but a dream. As I looked back upon the receding land, recollections of the past rushed through my mind in quick succession. From the treatment that I had received from the Americans as a victim of slavery, and the knowledge that I was at that time liable to be seized and again reduced to whips and chains, I had supposed that I would leave the country without any regret; but in this I was mistaken, for when I saw the last thread of communication cut off between me and the land, and the dim shores dying away in the distance, I almost regretted that I was not on shore.

An anticipated trip to a foreign country appears pleasant when talking about it, especially when surrounded by friends whom we love; but when we have left them all behind, it does not seem so pleasant. Whatever may be the fault of the government under which we live, and no matter how oppressive her laws may appear, yet we leave our native land (if such it be) with feelings akin to sorrow. With the steamer's powerful engine at work, and with a fair wind, we were speedily on the bosom of the Atlantic, which was as calm and as smooth as our own Hudson in its calmest aspect. We had on board above one hundred passengers, forty of whom were the "Viennese children"--a troop of dancers. The passengers represented several different nations, English, French, Spaniards, Africans, and Americans. One man who had the longest pair of mustaches that mortal man was ever doomed to wear, especially attracted my attention. He appeared to belong to no country in particular, but was yet the busiest man on board. After viewing for some time the many strange faces around me, I descended to the cabin to look after my luggage, which had been put hurriedly on board. I hope that all who take a trip of so great a distance may be as fortunate as I was, in being supplied with books to read on the voyage. My friends had furnished me with literature, from "Macaulay's History of England" to "Jane Eyre," so that I did not want for books to occupy my time.

A pleasant passage of about thirty hours, brought us to Halifax, at six o'clock in the evening. In company with my friend the President of the Oberlin Institute, I took a stroll through the town; and from what little I saw of the people in the streets, I am sure that the taking of the Temperance pledge would do them no injury. Our stay at Halifax was short. Having taken in a few sacks of coals, the mails, and a limited number of passengers, we were again out, and soon at sea. After a pleasant run of seven days more, and as I was lying in my bed, I heard the cry of "Land a-head." Although our passage had been unprecedentedly short, yet I need not inform you that this news was hailed with joy by all on board. For my own part, I was soon on deck. Away in the distance, and on our larboard quarter, were the grey hills of Ireland. Yes! we were in sight of the land of Emmett and O'Connell. While I rejoiced with the other passengers at the sight of land, and the near approach to the end of the voyage, I felt low spirited, because it reminded me of the great distance I was from home. But the experience of above twenty years' travelling, had prepared me to undergo what most persons must lay their account with, in visiting a strange country. This was the last day but one that we were to be on board; and as if moved by the sight of land, all seemed to be gathering their different things together--brushing up their old clothes and putting on their new ones, as if this would bring them any sooner to the end of their journey.

The last night on board was the most pleasant, apparently, that we had experienced; probably, because it was the last. The moon was in her meridian splendour, pouring her broad light over the calm sea; while near to us, on our starboard side, was a ship with her snow-white sails spread aloft, and stealing through the water like a thing of life. What can present a more picturesque view, than two vessels at sea on a moonlight night, and within a few rods of each other? With a gentle breeze, and the powerful engine at work, we seemed to be flying to the embrace of our British neighbours.

The next morning I was up before the sun, and found that we were within a few miles of Liverpool. The taking of a pilot on board at eleven o'clock, warned us to prepare to quit our ocean palace and seek other quarters. At a little past three o'clock, the ship cast anchor, and we were all tumbled, bag and baggage, into a small steamer, and in a few moments were at the door of the Custom-House. The passage had only been nine days and twenty-two hours, the quickest on record at that time, yet it was long enough. I waited nearly three hours before my name was called, and when it was, I unlocked my trunks and handed them over to one of the officers, whose dirty hands made no improvement on the work of the laundress. First one article was taken out, and then another, till an ***Iron Collar*** that had been worn by a female slave on the banks of the Mississippi, was hauled out, and this democratic instrument of torture became the centre of attraction; so much so, that instead of going on with the examination, all hands stopped to look at the "Negro Collar."

Several of my countrymen who were standing by, were not a little displeased at answers which I gave to questions on the subject of Slavery; but they held their peace. The interest created by the appearance of the Iron Collar, closed the examination of my luggage. As if afraid that they would find something more hideous, they put the Custom-House mark on each piece, and passed them out, and I was soon comfortably installed at Brown's Temperance Hotel, Clayton Square.

No person of my complexion can visit this country without being struck with the marked difference between the English and the Americans. The prejudice which I have experienced on all and every occasion in the United States, and to some extent on board the ***Canada***, vanished as soon as I set foot on the soil of Britain. In America I had been bought and sold as a slave, in the Southern States. In the so-called free States, I had been treated as one born to occupy an inferior position,--in steamers, compelled to take my fare on the deck; in hotels, to take my meals in the kitchen; in coaches, to ride on the outside; in railways, to ride in the "negro car;" and in churches, to sit in the "negro pew." But no sooner was I on British soil, than I was recognised as a man, and an equal. The very dogs in the streets appeared conscious of my manhood. Such is the difference, and such is the change that is brought about by a trip of nine days in an Atlantic steamer.

I was not more struck with the treatment of the people, than with the appearance of the great seaport of the world. The grey appearance of the stone piers and docks, the dark look of the magnificent warehouses, the substantial appearance of every thing around, causes one to think himself in a new world instead of the old. Every thing in Liverpool looks old, yet nothing is worn out. The beautiful villas on the opposite side of the river, in the vicinity of Birkenhead, together with the countless number of vessels in the river, and the great ships to be seen in the stream, give life and animation to the whole scene.

Every thing in and about Liverpool seems to be built for the future as well as the present. We had time to examine but few of the public buildings, the first of which was the Custom-House, an edifice that would be an ornament to any city in the world.

For the first time in my life, I can say "I am truly free." My old master may make his appearance here, with the Constitution of the United States in his pocket, the Fugitive Slave Law in one hand and the chains in the other, and claim me as his property, but all will avail him nothing. I can here stand and look the tyrant in the face, and tell him that I am his equal! England is, indeed, the "land of the free, and the home of the brave."

LETTER II.

Trip to Ireland--Dublin--Her Majesty's Visit--Illumination of the City--the Birth-Place of Thomas Moore--a Reception.

DUBLIN, *August 6*.

After remaining in Liverpool two days, I took passage in the little steamer *Adelaide* for this city. The wind being high on the night of our voyage, the vessel had scarcely got to sea ere we were driven to our berths; and though the distance from Liverpool to Dublin is short, yet, strange to say, I witnessed more effects of the sea and rolling of the steamer upon the passengers, than was to be seen during the whole of our voyage from America. We reached Kingstown, five miles below Dublin, after a passage of nearly fifteen hours, and were soon seated on a car, and on our way to the city. While coming into the bay, one gets a fine view of Dublin and the surrounding country. Few sheets of water make a more beautiful appearance than Dublin Bay. We found it as still and smooth as a mirror, with a soft mist on its surface--a strange contrast to the boisterous sea that we had left a moment before.

The curious phrases of the Irish sounded harshly upon my ear, probably, because they were strange to me. I lost no time on reaching the city in seeking out some to whom I had letters of introduction, one of whom gave me an invitation to make his house my home during my stay, an invitation which I did not think fit to decline.

Dublin, the Metropolis of Ireland, is a city of above two hundred thousand inhabitants, and is considered by the people of Ireland to be the second city in the British Empire. The Liffey, which falls into Dublin Bay a little below the Custom-House, divides the town into two nearly equal parts. The streets are--some of them--very fine, especially upper Sackville Street, in the centre of which stands a pillar erected to Nelson, England's most distinguished Naval Commander. The Bank of Ireland, to which I paid a visit, is a splendid building, and was formerly the Parliament House. This magnificent edifice fronts College Green, and near at hand stands a bronze statue of William III. The Bank and the Custom-House are two of the finest monuments of architecture in the city; the latter of which stands near the river Liffey, and its front makes an imposing appearance, extending to three hundred and seventy-five feet. It is built of Portland stone, and is adorned with a beautiful portico in the centre, consisting of four Doric columns supporting an enriched entablature, decorated with a group of figures in alto-relievo, representing Hibernia and Britannia presenting emblems of peace and liberty. A magnificent dome, supporting a cupola, on whose apex stands a colossal figure of Hope, rises nobly from the centre of the building to a height of one hundred and twenty-five feet. It is, withal, a fine specimen of what man can do.

From this noble edifice, we bent our steps to another part of the city, and soon found ourselves in the vicinity of St. Patrick's, where we had a heart-sickening view of the poorest of the poor. All the recollections of poverty which I had ever beheld, seemed to disappear in comparison with what was then before me. We passed a filthy and noisy market, where fruit and vegetable women were screaming and begging those passing by to purchase their commodities; while in and about the market-place were throngs of beggars fighting for rotten fruit, cabbage stocks, and even the very trimmings of vegetables. On the side walks, were great numbers hovering about the doors of the more wealthy, and following strangers, importuning them for "pence to buy bread." Sickly and emaciated-looking creatures, half naked, were at our heels at every turn. After passing through a half dozen, or more, of narrow and dirty streets, we returned to our lodgings, impressed with the idea that we had seen enough of the poor for one day.

In our return home, we passed through a respectable looking street, in which stands a small three storey brick building, which was pointed out to us as the birth-place of Thomas Moore, the poet. The following verse from one of Moore's poems was continually in my mind while viewing this house:--

> "Where is the slave, so lowly,
> Condemn'd to chains unholy,
> Who, could he burst
> His bonds at first,
> Would pine beneath them slowly?"

* * * * *

Yesterday was the Sabbath, but it had more the appearance of a holiday than a day of rest. It had been announced the day before, that the Royal fleet was expected, and at an early hour on Sunday, the entire town seemed to be on the move towards Kingstown, and as the family with whom I was staying followed the multitude, I was not inclined to remain behind, and so went with them. On reaching the station we found it utterly impossible to get standing room in any of the trains, much less a seat, and therefore determined to reach Kingstown under the plea of a morning's walk; and in this we were not alone, for during the walk of five miles the road was filled with thousands of pedestrians and a countless number of carriages, phaetons, and vehicles of a more humble order.

We reached the lower town in time to get a good dinner, and rest ourselves before going to make further searches for Her Majesty's fleet. At a little past four o'clock, we observed the multitude going towards the pier, a number of whom were yelling at the top of their voices, "It's coming, it's coming;" but on going to the quay, we found that a false alarm had been given. However, we had been on the look-out but a short time, when a column of smoke rising as it were out of the sea, announced that the Royal fleet was near at hand. The concourse in the vicinity of the pier was variously estimated at from eighty to one hundred thousand.

It was not long before the five steamers were entering the harbour, the one bearing Her Majesty leading the way. As each vessel had a number of distinguished persons on board, the people appeared to be at a loss to know which was the Queen; and as each party made its appearance on the promenade deck, they were received with great enthusiasm, the party having the best looking lady being received with the greatest applause. The Prince of Wales, and Prince Alfred, while crossing the deck were recognised and greeted with three cheers; the former taking off his hat and bowing to the people, showed that he had had some training as a public man although not ten years of age. But not so with Prince Alfred; for, when his brother turned to him and asked him to take off his hat and make a bow to the people, he shook his head and said, "No." This was received with hearty laughter by those on board, and was responded to by the thousands on shore. But greater applause was yet in store for the young prince; for the captain of the steamer being near by, and seeing that the Prince of Wales could not prevail on his brother to take off his hat, stepped up to him and undertook to take it off for him, when, seemingly to the delight of all, the prince put both hands to his head and held his hat fast. This was regarded as a sign of courage and future renown, and was received with the greatest enthusiasm--many crying out, "Good, good: he will make a brave king when his day comes."

After the greetings and applause had been wasted on many who had appeared on deck, all at once, as if by some magic power, we beheld a lady rather small in stature, with auburn or reddish hair, attired in a plain dress, and wearing a sky-blue bonnet, standing on the larboard paddle-box, by the side of a tall good-looking man, with mustaches. The thunders of applause that now rent the air, and cries of "The Queen, the Queen," seemed to set at rest the question of which was Her Majesty. But a few moments were allowed to the people to look at the Queen, before she again disappeared; and it was understood that she would not be seen again that evening. A rush was then made for the railway, to return to Dublin.

*   *   *   *   *

August 8.

Yesterday was a great day in Dublin. At an early hour the bells began their merry peals, and the people were soon seen in groups in the streets and public squares. The hour of ten was fixed for the procession to leave Kingstown, and it was expected to enter the city at eleven. The windows of the houses in the streets through which the Royal train was to pass, were at a premium, and seemed to find ready occupants.

Being invited the day previous to occupy part of a window in Upper Sackville Street, I was stationed at my allotted place, at an early hour, with an out-stretched neck and open eyes. My own colour differing from those about me, I attracted not a little attention from many; and often, when gazing down the street to see if the Royal procession was in sight, would find myself eyed by all around. But neither while at the window, or in the streets, was I once insulted. This was so unlike the American prejudice, that it seemed strange to me. It was near twelve o'clock before the procession entered Sackville Street, and when it did all eyes seemed to beam with delight. The first carriage contained only

Her Majesty and the Prince Consort; the second, the Royal children; and the third, the Lords in Waiting. Fifteen carriages were used by those that made up the Royal party. I had a full view of the Queen and all who followed in the train. Her Majesty--whether from actual love for her person, or the novelty of the occasion, I know not which--was received everywhere with the greatest enthusiasm. One thing, however, is certain, and that is--Queen Victoria is beloved by her subjects.

But the grand *fete* was reserved for the evening. Great preparations had been made to have a grand illumination on the occasion, and hints were thrown out that it would surpass anything ever witnessed in London. In this they were not far out of the way; for all who witnessed the scene admitted that it could scarcely have been surpassed. My own idea of an illumination, as I had seen it in the backwoods of my own native land, dwindled into nothing when compared with this magnificent affair.

In company with a few friends, and a lady under my charge, I undertook to pass through Sackville and one or two other streets, about eight o'clock in the evening, but we found it utterly impossible to proceed. Masses thronged the streets, and the wildest enthusiasm seemed to prevail. In our attempt to cross the bridge, we were wedged in and lost our companions; and on one occasion I was separated from the lady, and took shelter under a cart standing in the street. After being jammed and pulled about for nearly two hours, I returned to my lodgings, where I found part of my company, who had come in one after another. At eleven o'clock we had all assembled, and each told his adventures and "hairbreadth escapes;" and nearly every one had lost a pocket handkerchief or something of the kind: my own was among the missing. However, I lost nothing; for a benevolent lady, who happened to be one of the company, presented me with one which was of far more value than the one I had lost.

Every one appeared to enjoy the holiday which the Royal visit had caused. But the Irish are indeed a strange people. How varied their aspect--how contradictory their character. Ireland, the land of genius and degradation--of great resources and unparalleled poverty--noble deeds and the most revolting crimes--the land of distinguished poets, splendid orators, and the bravest of soldiers--the land of ignorance and beggary! Dublin is a splendid city, but its splendour is that of chiselled marble rather than real life. One cannot behold these architectural monuments without thinking of the great men that Ireland has produced. The names of Burke, Sheridan, Flood, Grattan, O'Connell, and Shiel, have become as familiar to the Americans as household words. Burke is known as the statesman; Sheridan for his great speech on the trial of Warren Hastings; Grattan for his eloquence; O'Connell as the agitator; and Shiel as the accomplished orator.

But of Ireland's sons, none stands higher in America than Thomas Moore, the Poet. The vigour of his sarcasm, the glow of his enthusiasm, the coruscations of his fancy, and the flashing of his wit, seem to be as well understood in the new world as the old; and the support which his pen has given to civil and religious liberty throughout the world, entitled the Minstrel of Erin to this elevated position.

Before leaving America I had heard much of the friends of my enslaved countrymen residing in Ireland; and the reception I met with on all hands while in public, satisfied me that what I had heard had not been exaggerated. To the Webbs, Allens, and Haughtons, of Dublin, the cause of the American slave is much indebted.

I quitted Dublin with a feeling akin to leaving my native land.

LETTER III.

Departure from Ireland--London--Trip to Paris--Paris--The Peace Congress: first day--Church of the Madeleine--Column Vendome--the French.

PARIS, *August 23*.

After a pleasant sojourn of three weeks in Ireland, I took passage in one of the mail steamers for Liverpool, and arriving there was soon on the road to the metropolis. The passage from Dublin to Liverpool was an agreeable one. The rough sea that we passed through on going to Ireland had given way to a dead calm, and our noble little steamer, on quitting the Dublin wharf, seemed to understand that she was to have it all her own way. During the first part of the evening, the boat appeared to feel her importance, and, darting through the water with majestic strides, she left behind her a dark cloud of smoke suspended in the air like a banner; while, far astern in the wake of the vessel, could be seen the rippled waves sparkling in the rays of the moon, giving strength and beauty to the splendour of the evening.

On reaching Liverpool, and partaking of a good breakfast, for which we paid double price, we proceeded to the railway station, and were soon going at a rate unknown to those accustomed to travel on one of our American railways. At a little past two o'clock in the afternoon, we saw in the distance the out-skirts of London. We could get but an indistinct view, which had the appearance of one architectural mass, extending all round to the horizon, and enveloped in a combination of fog and smoke; and towering above every other object to be seen, was the dome of St.

Paul's Cathedral.

A few moments more, and we were safely seated in a "Hansom's Patent," and on our way to Hughes's--one of the politest men of the George Fox stamp we have ever met. Here we found forty or fifty persons, who, like ourselves, were bound for the Peace Congress. The Sturges, the Wighams, the Richardsons, the Allens, the Thomases, and a host of others not less distinguished as friends of peace, were of the company--many of whom I had heard of, but none of whom I had ever seen; yet I was not an entire stranger to many, especially to the abolitionists. In company with a friend, I sallied forth after tea to take a view of the city. The evening was fine--the dense fog and smoke having to some extent passed away, left the stars shining brightly, while the gas light from the street lamps and the brilliant shop windows gave it the appearance of day-light in a new form. "What street is this?" we asked. "Cheapside," was the reply. The street was thronged, and every body seemed to be going at a rapid rate, as if there was something of importance at the end of the journey. Flying vehicles of every description passing each other with a dangerous rapidity, men with lovely women at their sides, children running about as if they had lost their parents--all gave a brilliancy to the scene scarcely to be excelled. If one wished to get jammed and pushed about, he need go no farther than Cheapside. But every thing of the kind is done with a degree of propriety in London, that would put the New Yorkers to blush. If you are run over in London, they "beg your pardon;" if they run over you in New York, you are "laughed at:" in London, if your hat is knocked off it is picked up and handed to you; if, in New York, you must pick it up yourself. There is a lack of good manners among Americans that is scarcely known or understood in Europe. Our stay in the great metropolis gave us but little opportunity of seeing much of the place; for in twenty-four hours after our arrival we joined the rest of the delegates, and started on our visit to our Gallic neighbours.

We assembled at the London Bridge Railway Station on Tuesday morning the 21st, a few minutes past nine, to the number of 600. The day was fine, and every eye seemed to glow with enthusiasm. Besides the delegates, there were probably not less than 600 more, who had come to see the company start. We took our seats and appeared to be waiting for nothing but the iron-horse to be fastened to the train, when all at once, we were informed that we must go to the booking-office and change our tickets. At this news every one appeared to be vexed. This caused great trouble; for on returning to the train many persons got into the wrong carriages; and several parties were separated from their friends, while not a few were calling out at the top of their voices, "Where is my wife? Where is my husband? Where is my luggage? Who's got my boy? Is this the right train?" "What is that lady going to do with all these children?" asked the guard. "Is she a delegate: are all the children delegates?" In the carriage where I had taken my seat was a good-looking lady who gave signs of being very much annoyed. "It is just so when I am going anywhere: I never saw the like in my life," said she. "I really wish I was at home again."

An hour had now elapsed, and we were still at the station. However, we were soon on our way, and going at express speed. In passing through Kent we enjoyed the scenery exceedingly, as the weather was altogether in our favour; and the drapery which nature hung on the trees, in the part through which we passed, was in all its gaiety. On our arrival at Folkstone, we found three steamers in readiness to convey the party to Boulogne. As soon as the train stopped, a general rush was made for the steamers; and in a very short time the one in which I had embarked was passing out of the harbour. The boat appeared to be conscious that we were going on a holy mission, and seemed to be proud of her load. There is nothing in this wide world so like a thing of life as a steamer, from the breathing of her steam and smoke, the energy of her motion, and the beauty of her shape; while the ease with which she is managed by the command of a single voice, makes her appear as obedient as the horse is to the rein.

When we were about half way between the two great European Powers, the officers began to gather the tickets. The first to whom he applied, and who handed out his "Excursion Ticket," was informed that we were all in the wrong boat. "Is this not one of the boats to take over the delegates?" asked a pretty little lady, with a whining voice. "No, Madam," said the captain. "You must look to the committee for your pay," said one of the company to the captain. "I have nothing to do with committees," the captain replied. "Your fare, Gentlemen, if you please."

Here the whole party were again thrown into confusion. "Do you hear that? We are in the wrong boat." "I knew it would be so," said the Rev. Dr. Ritchie, of Edinburgh. "It is indeed a pretty piece of work," said a plain-looking lady in a handsome bonnet. "When I go travelling again," said an elderly looking gent with an eye-glass to his face, "I will take the phaeton and old Dobbin." Every one seemed to lay the blame on the committee, and not, too, without some just grounds. However, Mr. Sturge, one of the committee, being in the boat with us, an arrangement was entered into, by which we were not compelled to pay our fare the second time.

As we neared the French coast, the first object that attracted our attention was the Napoleon Pillar, on the top of which is a statue of the Emperor in the Imperial robes. We landed, partook of refreshment that had been prepared for us, and again repaired to the railway station. The arrangements for leaving Boulogne were no better than those at London. But after the delay of another hour, we were again in motion.

It was a beautiful country through which we passed from Boulogne to Amiens. Straggling cottages which bespeak neatness and comfort abound on every side. The eye wanders over the diversified views with unabated pleasure, and rests in calm repose upon its superlative beauty. Indeed, the eye cannot but be gratified at viewing the entire country from the coast to the metropolis. Sparkling hamlets spring up as the steam horse speeds his way, at almost every point--showing the progress of civilization, and the refinement of the nineteenth century.

We arrived at Paris a few minutes past twelve o'clock at night, when, according to our tickets, we should have been there at nine. Elihu Burritt, who had been in Paris some days, and who had the arrangements there pretty much his own way, was at the station waiting the arrival of the train, and we had demonstrated to us, the best evidence that he understood his business. In no other place on the whole route had the affairs been so well managed; for we were seated in our respective carriages and our luggage placed on the top, and away we went to our hotels without the least difficulty or inconvenience. The champion of an "Ocean Penny Postage" received, as he deserved, thanks from the whole company for his admirable management.

The silence of the night was only disturbed by the rolling of the wheels of the omnibus, as we passed through the dimly lighted streets. Where, a few months before was to be seen the flash from the cannon and the musket, and the hearing of the cries and groans behind the barricades, was now the stillness of death--nothing save here and there a ***gens d'arme*** was to be seen going his rounds in silence.

The omnibus set us down at the hotel Bedford, Rue de L'Arend, where, although near one o'clock, we found a good supper waiting for us; and, as I was not devoid of an appetite, I did my share towards putting it out of the way.

The next morning I was up at an early hour, and out on the Boulevards to see what might be seen. As I was passing from the Bedford to the Place de La Concord, all at once, and as if by some magic power, I found myself in front of the most splendid edifice imaginable, situated at the end of the Rue Nationale. Seeing a number of persons entering the church at that early hour, and recognising among them my friend the President of the Oberlin (Ohio) Institute, and wishing not to stray too far from my hotel before breakfast, I followed the crowd and entered the building. The church itself consisted of a vast nave, interrupted by four pews on each side, fronted with lofty fluted Corinthian columns standing on pedestals, supporting colossal arches, bearing up cupolas, pierced with skylights and adorned with compartments gorgeously gilt; their corners supported with saints and apostles in ***alto relievo***. The walls of the church were lined with rich marble. The different paintings and figures, gave the interior an imposing appearance. On inquiry, I found that I was in the Church of the Madeleine. It was near this spot that some of the most interesting scenes occurred during the Revolution of 1848, which dethroned Louis Philippe. Behind the Madeleine is a small but well supplied market; and on an esplanade east of the edifice, a flower market is held on Tuesdays and Fridays.

* * * * *

The first session of the Peace Congress is over.

The Congress met this morning at 11 o'clock, in the Salle St. Cecile, Rue de la St. Lazare. The Parisians have no "Exeter Hall:" in fact, there is no private hall in the city of any size, save this, where such a meeting could be held. This hall has been fitted up for the occasion. The room is long, and at one end has a raised platform; and at the opposite end is a gallery, with seats raised one above another. On one side of the hall was a balcony with sofas, which were evidently the "reserved seats."

The hall was filled at an early hour with the delegates, their friends, and a good sprinkling of the French. Occasionally, small groups of gentlemen would make their appearance on the platform, until it soon appeared that there was little room left for others; and yet the officers of the Convention had not come in. The different countries were, many of them, represented here. England, France, Belgium, Germany, Switzerland, Greece, Spain, and the United States, had each their delegates. The Assembly began to give signs of impatience, when very soon the train of officials made their appearance amid great applause. Victor Hugo led the way, followed by M. Duguerry, cure of the Madeleine, Elihu Burritt, and a host of others of less note. Victor Hugo took the chair as President of the Congress, supported by Vice-presidents from the several nations represented. Mr. Richard, the Secretary, read a dry report of the names of societies, committees, &c., which was deemed the opening of the Convention.

The President then arose, and delivered one of the most impressive and eloquent appeals in favour of peace that could possibly be imagined. The effect produced upon the minds of all present was such as to make the author of "***Notre Dame de Paris***" a great favourite with the Congress. An English gentleman near me said to his friend, "I can't understand a word of what he says, but is it not good?" Victor Hugo concluded his speech amid the greatest enthusiasm on the part of the French, which was followed by hurrahs in the old English style. The Convention was successively addressed by the President of the Brussels Peace Society; President Mahan of the Oberlin (Ohio) Institute, U.S.; Henry Vincent; and Richard Cobden. The latter was not only the ***lion*** of the English delegation, but the great man of the Convention. When Mr. Cobden speaks, there is no want of hearers. The great power of this gentleman lies in his facts and his earnestness, for he cannot be called an eloquent speaker. Mr. Cobden addressed the Congress first in French, then in English; and, with the single exception of Mr. Ewart, M.P., was the only one of the English delegation that could speak to the French in their own language.

The Congress was brought to a close at five o'clock, when the numerous audience dispersed--the citizens to their homes, and the delegates to see the sights.

I was not a little amused at an incident that occurred at the close of the first session. On the passage from America, there were in the same steamer with me, several Americans, and among these, three or four appeared to be much annoyed at the fact that I was a passenger, and enjoying the company of white persons; and although I was not openly insulted, I very often heard the remark, that "That nigger had better be on his master's farm," and "What could the American Peace Society be thinking about to send a black man as a delegate to Paris." Well, at the close of the first sitting of the Convention, and just as I was leaving Victor Hugo, to whom I had been introduced by an M.P., I observed near me a gentleman with his hat in hand, whom I recognized as one of the passengers who had crossed the Atlantic with me in the ***Canada***, and who appeared to be the most horrified at having a negro for a fellow passenger. This gentleman, as I left M. Hugo, stepped up to me and said, "How do you do, Mr. Brown?" "You have the advantage of me," said I. "Oh, don't you know me; I was a fellow passenger with you from America; I wish you would give me an introduction to Victor Hugo and Mr. Cobden." I need not inform you that I declined introducing this pro-slavery American to these distinguished men. I only allude to this, to show what a change comes over the dreams of my white American brother, by crossing the ocean. The man who would not have been seen walking with me in the streets of New York, and who would not have shaken hands with me with a pair of tongs while on the passage from the United States, could come with hat in hand in Paris, and say, "I was your fellow-passenger." From the Salle de St. Cecile, I visited the Column Vendome, from the top of which I obtained a fine view of Paris and its environs. This is the Bunker Hill Monument of Paris. On the top of this pillar is a statue of the Emperor Napoleon, eleven feet high. The monument is built with stone, and the outside covered with a metallic composition, made of cannons, guns, spikes, and other warlike implements taken from the Russians and Austrians by Napoleon. Above 1200 cannons were melted down to help to create this monument of folly, to commemorate the success of the French arms in the German Campaign. The column is in imitation of the Trajan pillar at Rome, and is twelve feet in diameter at the base. The door at the bottom of the pillar, and where we entered, was decorated above with crowns of oak, surmounted by eagles, each weighing 500 lbs. The bas-relief of the shaft pursues a spiral direction to the capitol, and displays, in a chronological order, the principal actions of the French army, from the departure of the troops from Boulogne to the battle of Austerlitz. The figures are near three feet high, and their number said to be two thousand. This sumptuous monument stands on a plinth of polished granite, surmounted by an iron railing; and, from its size and position, has an imposing appearance when seen from any part of the city.

Everything here appears strange and peculiar--the people not less so than their speech. The horses, carriages, furniture, dress, and manners, are in keeping with their language. The appearance of the labourers in caps, resembling nightcaps, seemed particularly strange to me. The women without bonnets, and their caps turned the right side behind, had nothing of the look of our American women. The prettiest woman I ever saw was without a bonnet, walking on the Boulevards. While in Ireland, and during the few days I was in England, I was struck with the marked difference between the appearance of the women from those of my own country. The American women are too tall, too sallow, and too long-featured to be called pretty. This is most probably owing to the fact that in America the people come to maturity earlier than in most other countries.

My first night in Paris was spent with interest. No place can present greater street attractions than the Boulevards of Paris. The countless number of cafes, with tables before the doors, and these surrounded by men with long moustaches, with ladies at their sides, whose very smiles give indication of happiness, together with the sound of music from the gardens in the rear, tell the stranger that he is in a different country from his own.

LETTER IV.

Versailles--The Palace--Second Session of the Congress--Mr. Cobden--Henry Vincent--M. Girardin--Abbe Duguerry--Victor Hugo: his Speech.

VERSAILLES, *August 24*.

After the Convention had finished its sittings yesterday, I accompanied Mrs. M. C---- and sisters to Versailles, where they are residing during the summer. It was really pleasing to see among the hundreds of strange faces in the Convention, those distinguished friends of the slave from Boston.

Mrs. C----'s residence is directly in front of the great palace where so many kings have made their homes, the prince of whom was Louis XIV. The palace is now unoccupied. No ruler has dared to take up his residence here since Louis XVI. and Marie Antoinette were driven from it by the mob from Paris on the 8th of October, 1789. The town looks like the wreck of what it once was. At the commencement of the first revolution, it contained one hundred thousand inhabitants; now it has only about thirty thousand. It seems to be going back to what it was in the time of Louis XIII., when in 1624 he built a small brick chateau, and from it arose the magnificent palace which now stands here, and which attracts strangers to it from all parts of the world.

I arose this morning before the sun, and took a walk through the grounds of the Palace, and remained three hours among the fountains and statuary of this more than splendid place. But as I intend spending some days here, and shall have better opportunities of seeing and judging, I will defer my remarks upon Versailles for the present.

Yesterday was a great day in the Congress. The session was opened by a speech from M. Coquerel, the Protestant clergyman in Paris. His speech was received with much applause, and seemed to create great sensation in the Congress, especially at the close of his remarks, when he was seized by the hand by the Abbe Duguerry, amid the most deafening and enthusiastic applause of the entire multitude. The meeting was then addressed in English by a short gentleman, of florid complexion. His words seemed to come without the least difficulty, and his jestures, though somewhat violent, were evidently studied; and the applause with which he was greeted by the English delegation, showed that he was a man of no little distinction among them. His speech was one continuous flow of rapid, fervid eloquence, that seemed to fire every heart; and although I disliked his style, I was prepossessed in his favour. This was Henry Vincent, and his speech was in favour of disarmament.

Mr. Vincent was followed by M. Emile de Girardin, the editor of *La Presse*, in one of the most eloquent speeches that I ever heard; and his exclamation of "Soldiers of Peace," drew thunders of applause from his own countrymen. M. Girardin is not only the leader of the French press, but is a writer on politics of great distinction, and a leader of no inconsiderable party in the National Assembly; although still a young man, apparently not more than thirty-eight or forty years of age.

After a speech from Mr. Ewart, M.P., in French, and another from Mr.

Cobden in the same language, the Convention was brought to a close for the day. I spent the morning yesterday, in visiting some of the lions of the French capital, among which was the Louvre. The French Government having kindly ordered, that the members of the Peace Congress should be admitted free, and without ticket, to all the public works, I had nothing to do but present my card of membership, and was immediately admitted.

The first room I entered, was nearly a quarter of a mile in length; is known as the "Long Gallery," and contains some of the finest paintings in the world. On entering this superb palace, my first impression was, that all Christendom had been robbed, that the Louvre might make a splendid appearance. This is the Italian department, and one would suppose by its appearance that but few paintings had been left in Italy. The entrance end of the Louvre was for a long time in an unfinished state, but was afterwards completed by that master workman, the Emperor Napoleon. It was long thought that the building would crumble into decay, but the genius of the great Corsican rescued it from ruin.

During our walk through the Louvre, we saw some twenty or thirty artists copying paintings; some had their copies finished and were going out, others half done, while many had just commenced. I remained some minutes near a pretty French girl, who was copying a painting of a dog rescuing a child from a stream of water into which it had fallen.

I walked down one side of the hall and up the other, and was about leaving, when I was informed that this was only one room, and that a half-dozen more were at my service; but a clock on a neighbouring church reminded me that I must quit the Louvre for the Salle de St. Cecile.

* * * * *

This morning the Hall was filled at an early hour with rather a more fashionable looking audience than on any former occasion, and all appeared anxious for the Congress to commence its session, as it was understood to be the last day. After the reading of several letters from gentlemen, apologising for their not being able to attend, the speech of Elihu Burritt was read by a son of M. Coquerel. I felt somewhat astonished that my countryman, who was said to be master of fifty languages, had to get some one to read his speech in French.

The Abbe Duguerry now came forward amid great cheering, and said that "the eminent journalist, Girardin, and the great English logician, Mr. Cobden, had made it unnecessary for any further advocacy in that assembly of the Peace cause--that if the principles laid down in the resolutions were carried out, the work would be done. He said that the question of general pacification was built on truth--truth which emanated from God--and it were as vain to undertake to prevent air from expanding as to check the progress of truth. It must and would prevail."

A pale, thin-faced gentleman next ascended the platform (or tribune, as it was called) amid shouts of applause from the English, and began his speech in rather a low tone, when compared with the sharp voice of Vincent, or the thunder of the Abbe Duguerry. An audience is not apt to be pleased or even contented with an inferior speaker, when surrounded by eloquent men, and I looked every moment for manifestations of disapprobation, as I felt certain that the English delegation had made a mistake in applauding this gentleman who seemed to make such an unpromising beginning. But the speaker soon began to get warm on the subject, and even at times appeared as if he had spoken before. In a very short time, with the exception of his own voice, the stillness of death prevailed throughout the building. The speaker, in the delivery of one of the most logical speeches made in the Congress, and despite of his thin, sallow look, interested me much more than any whom I had before heard. Towards the close of his remarks, he was several times interrupted by manifestations of approbation; and finally concluded amid great cheering. I inquired the gentleman's name, and was informed that it was Edward Miall, editor of the ***Nonconformist***.

After speeches from several others, the great Peace Congress of 1849, which had brought men together from nearly all the governments of Europe, and many from America, was brought to a final close by a speech from the President, returning thanks for the honour that had been conferred upon him. He said, "My address shall be short, and yet I have to bid you adieu! How resolve to do so? Here, during three days, have questions of the deepest import been discussed, examined, probed to the bottom; and during these discussions, counsels have been given to governments which they will do well to profit by. If these days' sittings are attended with no other result, they will be the means of sowing in the minds of those present, gems of cordiality which must ripen into good fruit. England, France, Belgium, Europe, and America, would all be drawn closer by these sittings. Yet the moment to part has arrived, but I can feel that we are strongly united in heart. But before parting I may congratulate you and myself on the result of our proceedings. We have been all joined together without distinction of country; we have all been united in one common feeling during our three days' communion. The good work cannot go back, it must advance, it must be accomplished. The course of the future may be judged of by the sound of the footsteps of the past. In the course of that day's discussion, a reminiscence had been handed up to one of the speakers, that this was the anniversary of the dreadful massacre of St. Bartholomew: the rev. gentleman who was speaking turned away from the thought of that sanguinary scene with pious horror, natural to his sacred calling. But I, who may boast of firmer nerve, I take up the remembrance. Yes, it was on this day, two hundred and seventy-seven years ago, that Paris was roused from slumber by the sound of that bell which bore the name of ***cloche d'argent***. Massacre was on foot, seeking with keen eye for its victim--man was busy in slaying man. That slaughter was called forth by mingled passions of the worst description. Hatred of all kinds was there urging on the slayer--hatred of a religious, a political, a personal character. And yet on the anniversary of that same day of horror, and in that very city whose blood was flowing like water, has God this day given a rendezvous to men of peace, whose wild tumult is transformed into order, and animosity into love. The stain of blood is blotted out, and in its place beams forth a ray of holy light. All distinctions are removed, and Papist and Huguenot meet together in friendly communion. (Loud cheers.) Who that thinks of these amazing changes can doubt of the progress that has been made? But whoever denies the force of progress must deny God, since progress is the boon of Providence, and emanated from the great Being above. I feel gratified for the change that has been effected, and, pointing solemnly to the past, I say let this day be ever held memorable--let the 24th of August, 1572, be remembered only for the purpose of being compared with the 24th of August, 1849; and when we think of the latter, and ponder over the high purpose to which it has been devoted--the advocacy of the principles of peace--let us not be so wanting in reliance on Providence as to doubt for one moment of the eventful success of our holy cause."

The most enthusiastic cheers followed this interesting speech. A vote of thanks to the government, and three times three cheers, with Mr. Cobden as "fugleman," ended the great Peace Congress of 1849.

Time for separating had arrived, yet all seemed unwilling to leave the place, where for three days men of all creeds and of no creed had met upon one common platform. In one sense the meeting was a glorious one--in another, it was mere child's play; for the Congress had been restricted to the discussion of certain topics. They were permitted to dwell on the blessings of peace, but were not allowed to say anything about the very subjects above all others that should have been brought before the Congress. A French army had invaded Rome and put down the friends of political and religious freedom, yet not a word was said in reference to it. The fact is, the Committee permitted the Congress to be *gagged*, before it had met. They put padlocks upon their own mouths, and handed the keys to the government. And this was sorely felt by many of the speakers. Richard Cobden, who had thundered his anathemas against the Corn Laws of his own country, and against wars in every clime, had to sit quiet in his fetters. Henry Vincent, who can make a louder speech in favour of peace, than almost any other man, and whose denunciations of "all war," have gained him no little celebrity with peace men, had to confine himself to the blessings of peace. Oh! how I wished for a Massachusetts atmosphere, a New England Convention platform, with Wendell Phillips as the speaker, before that assembled multitude from all parts of the world.

But the Congress is over, and cannot now be made different; yet it is to be hoped that neither the London Peace Committee, nor any other men having the charge of getting up such another great meeting, will commit such an error again.

LETTER V.

M. de Tocqueville's Grand Soiree--Madame de Tocqueville--Visit of the Peace Delegates to Versailles--The Breakfast--Speechmaking--The Trianons--Waterworks--St. Cloud--The Fete.

VERSAILLES, *August 24*.

The day after the close of the Congress, the delegates and their friends were invited to a soiree by M. de Tocqueville, Minister for Foreign

Affairs, to take place on the next evening (Saturday); and, as my coloured face and curly hair did not prevent my getting an invitation, I was present with the rest of my peace brethren.

Had I been in America, where colour is considered a crime, I would not have been seen at such a gathering, unless as a servant. In company with several delegates, we left the Bedford Hotel for the mansion of the Minister of Foreign Affairs; and, on arriving, we found a file of soldiers drawn up before the gate. This did not seem much like peace: however, it was merely done in honour of the company. We entered the building through massive doors and resigned ourselves into the hands of good-looking waiters in white wigs; and, after our names were duly announced, were passed from room to room till I was presented to Madame de Tocqueville, who was standing near the centre of the large drawing-room, with a bouquet in her hand. I was about passing on, when the gentleman who introduced me intimated that I was an "American slave." At the announcement of this fact the distinguished lady extended her hand and gave me a cordial welcome--at the same time saying, "I hope you feel yourself free in Paris." Having accepted an invitation to a seat by the lady's side, who seated herself on a sofa, I was soon what I most dislike, "the observed of all observers." I recognised among many of my own countrymen, who were gazing at me, the American Consul, Mr. Walsh. My position did not improve his looks. The company present on this occasion were variously estimated at from one thousand to fifteen hundred. Among these were the Ambassadors from the different countries represented at the French metropolis, and many of the *elite* of Paris. One could not but be interested with the difference in dress, looks, and manners of this assemblage of strangers whose language was as different as their general appearance. Delight seemed to beam in every countenance as the living stream floated from one room to another. The house and gardens were illuminated in the most gorgeous manner. Red, yellow, blue, green, and many other coloured lamps, suspended from the branches of the trees in the gardens, gave life and animation to the whole scene out of doors. The soiree passed off satisfactorily to all parties; and by twelve o'clock I was again at my Hotel.

* * * * *

Through the politeness of the government the members of the Congress have not only had the pleasure of seeing all the public works free, and without special ticket, but the palaces of Versailles and St. Cloud, together with their splendid grounds, have been thrown open, and the water-works set to playing in both places. This mark of respect for the Peace movement is commendable in the French; and were I not such a strenuous friend of free speech, this act would cause me to overlook the padlocks that the government put upon our lips in the Congress.

Two long trains left Paris at nine o'clock for Versailles; and at each of the stations the company were loudly cheered by the people who had assembled to see them pass. At Versailles, we found thousands at the station, who gave us a most enthusiastic welcome. We were blessed with a goodly number of the fair sex, who always give life and vigour to such scenes. The train had scarcely stopped, ere the great throng were wending their ways in different directions, some to the cafes to get what an early start prevented their getting before leaving Paris, and others to see the soldiers who were on review. But most bent their steps towards the great palace.

At eleven o'clock we were summoned to the ***dejeuner***, which had been prepared by the English delegates in honour of their American friends. About six hundred sat down at the tables. Breakfast being ended, Mr. Cobden was called to the chair, and several speeches were made. Many who had not an opportunity to speak at the Congress, thought this a good chance; and the written addresses which had been studied during the passage from America, with the hope that they would immortalize their authors before the great Congress, were produced at the breakfast table.

But speech-making was not the order of the day. Too many thundering addresses had been delivered in the Salle de St. Cecile, to allow the company to sit and hear dryly written and worse delivered speeches in the Teniscourt.

There was no limited time given to the speakers, yet no one had been on his feet five minutes, before the cry was heard from all parts of the house, "Time, time." One American was hissed down, another took his seat with a red face, and a third opened his bundle of paper, looked around at the audience, made a bow, and took his seat amid great applause. Yet some speeches were made, and to good effect, the best of which was by Elihu Burritt, who was followed by the Rev. James Freeman Clark. I regretted very much that the latter did not deliver his address before the Congress, for he is a man of no inconsiderable talent, and an acknowledged friend of the slave.

The cry of "The water-works are playing," "The water is on," broke up the meeting, without even a vote of thanks to the Chairman; and the whole party were soon revelling among the fountains and statues of Louis XIV. Description would fail to give a just idea of the grandeur and beauty of this splendid place. I do not think that any thing can surpass the fountain of Neptune, which stands near the Grand Trianon. One may easily get lost in wandering through the grounds of Versailles, but he will always be in sight of some life-like statue. These monuments, erected to gratify the fancy of a licentious king, make their appearance at every turn. Two lions, the one overturning a wild boar, the other a wolf, both the production of Fillen, pointed out to us the fountain of Diana. But I will not attempt to describe to you any of the very beautiful sculptured gods and goddesses here.

With a single friend I paid a visit to the two Trianons. The larger was, we were told, just as king Louis Philippe left it. One room was splendidly fitted up for the reception of Her Majesty Queen Victoria;

who, it appeared, had promised a visit to the French Court; but the French Monarch ran away from his throne before the time arrived. The Grand Trianon is not larger than many noblemen's seats that may be seen in a day's ride through any part of the British empire. The building has only a ground floor, but its proportions are very elegant.

We next paid our respects to the Little Trianon. This appears to be the most Republican of any of the French palaces. I inspected this little palace with much interest, not more for its beauty than because of its having been the favourite residence of that purest of Princesses, best of Queens, and most affectionate of mothers, Marie Antoinette. The grounds and building may be said to be only a palace in miniature, and this makes it still a more lovely spot. The building consists of a square pavilion two stories high, and separated entirely from the accessory buildings, which are on the left, and among them a pretty chapel. But a wish to be with the multitude, who were roving among the fountains, cut short my visit to the trianons.

The day was very fine, and the whole party seemed to enjoy it. It was said that there were more than one hundred thousand persons at Versailles during the day. The company appeared to lose themselves with the pleasure of walking among the trees, flower beds, fountains, and statues. I met more than one wife seeking a lost husband, and *vice versa*. Many persons were separated from their friends and did not meet them again till at the hotels in Paris. In the train returning to Paris, an old gentleman who was seated near me said, "I would rest contented if I thought I should ever see my wife again!"

At four o'clock we were *en route* to St. Cloud, the much loved and favourite residence of the Emperor Napoleon. It seemed that all Paris had come out to St. Cloud to see how the English and Americans would enjoy the playing of the water-works. Many kings and rulers of the French have made St. Cloud their residence, but none have impressed their images so indelibly upon it as Napoleon. It was here he was first elevated to power, and here Josephine spent her most happy hours.

The apartments where Napoleon was married to Marie Louise; the private rooms of Josephine and Marie Antoinette, were all in turn shown to us. While standing on the balcony looking at Paris one cannot wonder that the Emperor should have selected this place as his residence, for a more lovely spot cannot be found than St. Cloud.

The palace is on the side of a hill, two leagues from Paris, and so situated that it looks down upon the French capital. Standing, as we did, viewing Paris from St. Cloud, and the setting sun reflecting upon the domes, spires, and towers of the city of fashion, made us feel that this was the place from which the monarch should watch his subjects. From the hour of arrival at St. Cloud till near eight o'clock, we were either inspecting the splendid palace or roaming the grounds and gardens, whose beautiful walks and sweet flowers made it appear a very Paradise on earth.

At eight o'clock the water-works were put in motion, and the variagated lamps with their many devices, displaying flowers, stars, and wheels, all with a brilliancy that can scarcely be described, seemed to throw everything in the shade we had seen at Versailles. At nine o'clock the train was announced, and after a good deal of jamming and pushing about, we were again on the way to Paris.

LETTER VI.

The Tuileries--Place de la Concorde--The Egyptian Obelisk--Palais Royal--Residence of Robespierre--A Visit to the Room in which Charlotte Corday killed Marat--Church de Notre Dame--Palais de Justice--Hotel des Invalids--National Assembly--The Elysee.

PARIS, *August 28*.

Yesterday morning I started at an early hour for the Palace of the Tuileries. A show of my card of membership of the Congress (which had carried me through so many of the public buildings) was enough to gain me immediate admission. The attack of the mob on the palace, on the 20th of June, 1792, the massacre of the Swiss guard on the 10th of August of the same year, the attack by the people in July 1830, together with the recent flight of king Louis Philippe and family, made me anxious to visit the old pile.

We were taken from room to room, until the entire building had been inspected. In front of the Tuileries, are a most magnificent garden and grounds. These were all laid out by Louis XIV., and are left nearly as they were during that monarch's reign. Above fifty acres surrounded by an iron rail fence, fronts the Place de la Concorde, and affords a place of promenade for the Parisians. I walked the pleasing grounds, and saw hundreds of well dressed persons walking under the shade of the great chestnuts, or sitting on chairs which were kept to let at two sous a piece. Near by is the Place de Carrousel, noted for its historical remembrances. Many incidents connected with the several revolutions occurred here, and it is pointed out as the place where Napoleon reviewed that formidable army of his before its departure for Russia.

From the Tuileries, I took a stroll through the Place de la Concorde, which has connected with it so many acts of cruelty, that it made me shudder as I passed over its grounds. As if to take from one's mind the old associations of this place, the French have erected on it, or rather given a place to, the celebrated obelisk of Luxor, which now is the chief attraction on the grounds. The obelisk was brought from Egypt at an enormous expense; for which purpose a ship was built, and several hundred men employed above three years in its removal. It is formed of the finest red syenite, and covered on each side with three lines of hieroglyphic inscriptions, commemorative of Sesostris--the middle lines being the most deeply cut and most carefully finished; and the characters altogether number more than 1600. The obelisk is of a single stone, is 72 feet in height, weighs 500,000 lbs., and stands on a block of granite that weighs 250,000 lbs. He who can read Latin will see that the monument tells its own story, but to me its characters were all blank.

It would be tedious to follow the history of this old and venerated stone, which was taken from the quarry 1550 years before the birth of Christ; placed in Thebes; its removal; the journey to the Nile, and down the Nile; thence to Cherbourg, and lastly its arrival in Paris on the 23d of December, 1833--just one year before I escaped from slavery. The obelisk was raised on the spot where it now stands, on the 25th of October, 1836, in the presence of Louis Philippe and amid the greetings of 160,000 persons.

Having missed my dinner, I crossed over to the Palais Royal, to a dining saloon, and can assure you that a better dinner may be had there for five francs, than can be got in New York for twice that sum, and especially if the person who wants the dinner is a coloured man. I found no prejudice against my complexion in the Palais Royal.

Many of the rooms in this once abode of Royalty, are most splendidly furnished, and decorated with valuable pictures. The likenesses of Madame de Stael, J.J. Rousseau, Cromwell, and Francis I., are among them.

*   *   *   *   *

After several unsuccessful attempts to-day, in company with R.D. Webb, Esq., to seek out the house where once resided the notorious Robespierre, I was fortunate enough to find it, but not until I had lost the company of my friend. The house is No. 396, Rue St. Honore, opposite the Church of the Assumption. It stands back, and is reached by entering a court. During the first revolution it was occupied by M. Duplay, with whom Robespierre lodged. The room used by the great man of the revolution, was pointed out to me. It is small, and the ceiling low, with two windows looking out upon the court. The pin upon which the blue coat once hung, is still in the wall. While standing there, I could almost imagine that I saw the great "Incorruptible," sitting at the small table composing those speeches which gave him so much power and influence in the Convention and the Clubs.

Here, the disciple of Rousseau sat and planned how he should outdo his enemies and hold on to his friends. From this room he went forth, followed by his dog Brunt, to take his solitary walk in a favourite and neighbouring field, or to the fiery discussions of the National Convention. In the same street, is the house in which Madame Roland--one of Robespierre's victims--resided.

A view of the residence of one of the master spirits of the French revolution inclined me to search out more, and therefore I proceeded to the old town, and after winding through several small streets--some of them so narrow as not to admit more than one cab at a time--I found myself in the Rue de L'Ecole de Medecine, and standing in front of house No. 20. This was the residence, during the early days of the revolution, of that bloodthirsty demon in human form, Marat.

I said to a butcher, whose shop was underneath, that I wanted to see La Chambre de Marat. He called out to the woman of the house to know if I could be admitted, and the reply was, that the room was used as a sleeping apartment, and could not be seen.

As this was private property, my blue card of membership to the Congress was not available. But after slipping a franc into the old lady's hand, I was informed that the room was now ready. We entered a court and ascended a flight of stairs, the entrance to which is on the right; then crossing to the left, we were shown into a moderate-sized room on the first floor, with two windows looking out upon a yard. Here it was where the "Friend of the People" (as he styled himself,) sat and wrote those articles that appeared daily in his journal, urging the people to "hang the rich upon lamp posts." The place where the bath stood, in which he was bathing at the time he was killed by Charlotte Corday, was pointed out to us; and even something representing an old stain of blood was shown as the place where he was laid when taken out of the bath. The window, behind whose curtains the heroine hid, after she had plunged the dagger into the heart of the man whom she thought was the cause of the shedding of so much blood by the guillotine, was pointed out with a seeming degree of pride by the old woman.

With my Guide Book in hand, I again went forth to "hunt after new fancies."

*　　*　　*　　*　　*

After walking over the ground where the guillotine once stood, cutting off its hundred and fifty heads per day, and then visiting the place where some of the chief movers in that sanguinary revolution once lived, I felt little disposed to sleep, when the time for it had arrived. However, I was out this morning at an early hour, and on the Champs Elysees; and again took a walk over the place where the guillotine stood, when its fatal blade was sending so many unprepared spirits into eternity. When standing here, you have the Palace of the Tuileries on one side, the arch on the other; on a third, the classic Madeleine; and on the fourth, the National Assembly. It caused my blood to chill, the idea of being on the identical spot where the heads of Louis XVI. and his Queen, after being cut off, were held up to satisfy the blood-thirsty curiosity of the two hundred thousand persons that were assembled on the Place de la Revolution. Here Royal blood flowed as it never did before or since. The heads of patricians and plebians, were thrown into the same basket, without any regard to birth or station. Here Robespierre and Danton had stood again and again, and looked their victims in the face as they ascended the scaffold; and here, these same men had to mount the very scaffold that they had erected for others. I wandered up the Seine, till I found myself looking at the statue of Henry the IV. over the principal entrance of the Hotel de Ville. When we take into account the connection of the Hotel de Ville with the different revolutions, we must come to the conclusion, that it is one of the most remarkable buildings in Paris. The room was pointed out where Robespierre held his counsels, and from the windows of which he could look out upon the Place de Greve, where the guillotine stood before its removal to the Place de la Concorde. The room is large, with gilded hangings, splendid old-fashioned chandeliers, and a chimney-piece with fine antiquated carvings, that give it a venerable appearance. Here Robespierre not only presided at the counsels that sent hundreds to the guillotine; but from this same spot, he, with his brother St. Just and others, were dragged before the Committee of Public Safety, and thence to the guillotine, and justice and revenge satisfied.

The window from which Lafayette addressed the people in 1830, and presented to them Louis Philippe, as the king, was shown to us. Here the poet, statesman, philosopher and orator, Lamartine, stood in February 1848, and, by the power of his eloquence, succeeded in keeping the people quiet. Here he forced the mob, braved the bayonets presented to his breast, and, by his good reasoning, induced them to retain the tri-coloured flag, instead of adopting the red flag, which he considered the emblem of blood.

Lamartine is a great heroic genius, dear to liberty and to France; and successive generations, as they look back upon the revolution of 1848, will recall to memory the many dangers which nothing but his dauntless courage warded off. The difficulties which his wisdom surmounted, and the good service that he rendered to France, can never be adequately estimated or too highly appreciated. It was at the Hotel de Ville that the Republic of 1848 was proclaimed to the people.

I next paid my respects to the Column of July that stands on the spot formerly occupied by the Bastile. It is 163 feet in height, and on the top is the Genius of Liberty, with a torch in his right hand, and in the left a broken chain. After a fatiguing walk up a winding stair, I obtained a splendid view of Paris from the top of the column.

I thought I should not lose the opportunity of seeing the Church de Notre Dame while so near to it, and, therefore, made it my next rallying point. No edifice connected with religion has had more interesting incidents occurring in it than this old church. Here Pope Pius VII. placed the Imperial Crown on the head of the Corsican--or rather Napoleon took the Crown from his hands and placed it on his own head. Satan dragging the wicked to ----; the rider on the red horse at the opening of the second seal; the blessedness of the saints; and several other striking sculptured figures were among the many curiosities in this splendid place. A hasty view from the gallery concluded my visit to the Notre Dame.

Leaving the old church I strayed off in a direction towards the Seine, and passed by an old looking building of stately appearance, and recognised, among a throng passing in and out, a number of the members of the Peace Congress. I joined a party entering, and was soon in the presence of men with gowns on, and men with long staffs in their hands--and on inquiry found that I was in the Palais de Justice; beneath which is the Conciergerie, a noted prison. Louis XVI. and Marie Antoinette were tried and condemned to death here.

A bas-relief, by Cortat, representing Louis in conference with his Counsel, is here seen. But I had visited too many places of interest during the day to remain long in a building surrounded by officers of justice, and took a stroll upon the Boulevards.

The Boulevards may be termed the Regent Street of Paris, or a New Yorker would call them Broadway. While passing a cafe, my German friend Faigo, whose company I had enjoyed during the passage from America, recognised me, and I sat down and took a cup of delicious coffee for the first time on the side walk, in sight of hundreds who were passing up and down the street every hour. From three till eleven o'clock, P.M., the Boulevards are lined with men and women sitting before the doors of the saloons drinking their coffee or wines, or both at the same time, as fancy may dictate. All Paris appeared to be on the Boulevards, and looking as if the great end of this life was enjoyment.

*   *   *   *   *

Anxious to see as much as possible of Paris in the limited time I had to stay in it, I hired a cab yesterday morning and commenced with the Hotel des Invalids, a magnificent building, within a few minutes' walk of the National Assembly. On each side of the entrance gate are figures representing nations conquered by Louis XIV., with colossal statues of

Mars and Minerva. The dome on the edifice is the loftiest in Paris--the height from the ground being 323 feet.

Immediately below the dome is the tomb of the man at whose word the world turned pale. A statue of the Emperor Napoleon stands in the second piazza, and is of the finest bronze.

This building is the home of the pensioned soldiers of France. It was enough to make one sick at the idea of war, to look upon the mangled bodies of these old soldiers. Men with arms and no legs; others had legs but no arms; some with canes and crutches, and some wheeling themselves about in little hand carts. About three thousand of the decayed soldiers were lodged in the Hotel des Invalids, at the time of my visit. Passing the National Assembly on my return, I spent a moment or two in it. The interior of this building resembles an amphitheatre. It is constructed to accommodate 900 members, each having a separate desk. The seat upon which the Duchesse of Orleans, and her son, the Comte de Paris, sat, when they visited the National Assembly after the flight of Louis Philippe, was shown with considerable alacrity. As I left the building, I heard that the President of the Republic was on the point of leaving the Elysee for St. Cloud, and with the hope of seeing the "Prisoner of Ham," I directed my cabman to drive me to the Elysee.

In a few moments we were between two files of soldiers, and entering the gates of the palace. I called out to the driver and told him to stop; but I was too late, for we were now in front of the massive doors of the palace, and a liveried servant opened the cab door, bowed, and asked if I had an engagement with the President. You may easily "guess" his surprise when I told him no. In my best French, I asked the cabman why he had come to the palace, and was answered, "You told me to." By this time a number had gathered round, all making inquiries as to what I wanted. I told the driver to retrace his steps, and, amid the shrugs of their shoulders, the nods of their heads, and the laughter of the soldiers, I left the Elysee without even a sight of the President's mustaches for my trouble. This was only one of the many mistakes I made while in Paris.

LETTER VII.

The Chateau at Versailles--Private apartments of Marie Antoinette--The Secret Door--Paintings of Raphael and David--Arc de Triomphe--Beranger the Poet.

VERSAILLES, *August 31*.

Here I am, within ten leagues of Paris, spending the time pleasantly in viewing the palace and grounds of the great Chateau of Louis XIV. Fifty-seven years ago, a mob, composed of men, women, and boys, from Paris, stood in front of this palace and demanded that the king should go with them to the capital. I have walked over the same ground where the one hundred thousand stood on that interesting occasion. I have been upon the same balcony, and stood by the window from which Maria Antoinette looked out upon the mob that were seeking her life.

Anxious to see as much of the palace as I could, and having an offer of the company of my young friend, Henry G. Chapman, to go through the palace with me, I set out early yesterday morning, and was soon in the halls that had often been trod by Royal feet. We passed through the private, as well as the public, apartments, through the secret door by which Marie Antoinette had escaped from the mob of 1792, and viewed the room in which her faithful guards were killed, while attempting to save their Royal mistress. I took my seat in one of the little parlour carriages that had been used in days of yore for the Royal children; while my friend, H.G. Chapman, drew me across the room. The superb apartments are not now in use. Silence is written upon these walls, although upon them are suspended the portraits of men of whom the world has heard.

Paintings, representing Napoleon in nearly all his battles, are here seen; and wherever you see the Emperor, there you will also find Murat, with his white plume waving above. Callot's painting of the battle of Marengo, Hue's of the retaking of Genoa, and Bouchat's of the 18th Brumaire, are of the highest order; while David has transmitted his fame to posterity, by his splendid painting of the Coronation of Napoleon and Josephine in Notre Dame. When I looked upon the many beautiful paintings of the last named artist, that adorn the halls of Versailles, I did not wonder that his fame should have saved his life, when once condemned and sentenced to death during the reign of terror. The guillotine was robbed of its intended victim, but the world gained a great painter. As Boswell transmitted his own name to posterity with his life of Johnson, so has David left his, with the magnificent paintings that are now suspended upon the walls of the palaces of the Louvre, the Tuileries, St. Cloud, Versailles, and even the little Elysee.

After strolling from room to room, we found ourselves in the Salle du Sacre, Diane, Salon de Mars, de Mercure, and d'Apollon. I gazed with my eyes turned to the ceiling till I was dizzy. The Salon de la Guerre is covered with the most beautiful representations that the mind of man could conceive, or the hand accomplish. Louis XIV. is here in all his glory. No Marie Antoinette will ever do the honours in these halls again.

After spending a whole day in the Palace and several mornings in the Gardens, I finally bid adieu to the bronze statue of Louis XIV. that stands in front of the Palace, and left Versailles, probably for ever.

*   *   *   *   *

PARIS, *September 2*.

I am now on the point of quitting the French Metropolis. I have occupied the last two days in visiting places of note in the city. I could not resist the inclination to pay a second visit to the Louvre. Another hour was spent in strolling through the Italian Hall and viewing the master-workmanship of Raphael, the prince of painters. Time flies, even in such a place as the Louvre with all its attractions; and before I had seen half that I wished, a ponderous clock near by reminded me of an engagement, and I reluctantly tore myself from the splendours of the place.

During the rest of the day I visited the Jardin des Plantes, and spent an hour and a half pleasantly in walking among plants, flowers, and in fact everything that could be found in any garden in France. From this place we passed by the column of the Bastile, and paid our respects to the Bourse, or Exchange, one of the most superb buildings in the city. The ground floor and sides of the Bourse, are of fine marble, and the names of the chief cities in the world are inscribed on the medallions, which are under the upper cornice. The interior of the edifice has a most splendid appearance as you enter it.

The Cemetery of Pere la Chaise was too much talked of by many of our party at the Hotel for me to pass it by, so I took it after the Bourse. Here lie many of the great marshals of France--the resting place of each marked by the monument that stands over it, except one, which is marked only by a weeping willow and a plain stone at its head. This is the grave of Marshal Ney. I should not have known that it was his, but some unknown hand had written with black paint, "Bravest of the Brave," on the unlettered stone that stands at the head of the man who followed Napoleon through nearly all his battles, and who was shot after the occupation of Paris by the allied army. Peace to his ashes. During my ramble through this noted place, I saw several who were hanging fresh wreaths of everlasting flowers on the tombs of the departed.

A ride in an omnibus down the Boulevards, and away up the Champs Elysees, brought me to the Arc de Triomphe; and after ascending a flight of one hundred and sixty-one steps, I was overlooking the city of statuary. This stupendous monument was commenced by Napoleon in 1806; and in 1811 it had only reached the cornice of the base, where it stopped, and it was left for Louis Philippe to finish. The first stone of this monument was laid on the 15th of August, 1806, the birth-day of the man whose battles it was intended to commemorate. A model of the arch was erected for Napoleon to pass through as he was entering the city with Maria Louisa, after their marriage. The inscriptions on the monument are many, and the different scenes here represented are all of the most exquisite workmanship. The genius of War is summoning the obedient nations to battle. Victory is here crowning Napoleon after his great success in 1810. Fame stands here recording the exploits of the warrior, while conquered cities lie beneath the whole. But it would take more time than I have at command to give anything like a description of this magnificent piece of architecture.

That which seems to take most with Peace Friends, is the portion representing an old man taming a bull for agricultural labour; while a young warrior is sheathing his sword, a mother and children sitting at his feet, and Minerva crowned with laurels, stands shedding her protecting influence over them. The erection of this regal monument is wonderful, to hand down to posterity the triumphs of the man whom we first hear of as a student in the military school at Brienne, whom in 1784 we see in the Ecole Militaire, founded by Louis XV. in 1751; whom again we find at No. 5, Quai de Court, near Rue de Mail; and in 1794 as a lodger at No. 19, Rue de la Michandere. From this he goes to the Hotel Mirabeau, Rue du Dauphin, where he resided when he defeated his enemies on the 13th Vendimaire. The Hotel de la Colonade, Rue Neuve des Capuchins is his next residence, and where he was married to Josephine. From this hotel he removed to his wife's dwelling in the Rue Chanteriene, No. 52. In 1796 the young general started for Italy, where his conquests paved the way for the ever memorable 18th Brumaire, that made him dictator of France. Napoleon was too great now to be satisfied with private dwellings, and we next trace him to the Elysee, St. Cloud, Versailles, the Tuileries, Fontainbleau, and finally, came his decline, which I need not relate to you.

After visiting the Gobelins, passing through its many rooms, seeing here and there a half-finished piece of tapestry; and meeting a number of the members of the late Peace Congress, who, like myself had remained behind to see more of the beauties of the French capital than could be overtaken during the Convention week. I accepted an invitation to dine with a German gentleman at the Palais Royal, and was soon revelling amid the luxuries of the table. I was glad that I had gone to the Palais Royal, for here I had the honour of an introduction to M. Beranger, the poet; and although I had to converse with him through an interpreter, I enjoyed his company very much. "The people's poet," as he is called, is apparently about seventy years of age, bald on the top of the head, and rather corpulent, but of active look, and in the enjoyment of good health. Few writers in France have done better service to the cause of political and religious freedom, than Pierre Jean de Beranger. He is the dauntless friend and advocate of the down-trodden poor and oppressed, and has often incurred the displeasure of the Government by the arrows that he has thrown into their camp. He felt what he wrote; it came straight from his heart, and went directly to the hearts of the people. He expressed himself strongly opposed to slavery, and said, "I don't see how the Americans can reconcile slavery with their professed love of freedom." Dinner out of the way, a walk through the different apartments, and a stroll over the court, and I bade adieu to the Palais Royal, satisfied that I should partake of many worse dinners than I had helped to devour that day.

Few nations are more courteous than the French. Here the stranger, let him come from what country he may, and be ever so unacquainted with the people and language, he is sure of a civil reply to any question that he may ask. With the exception of the egregious blunder I have mentioned of the cabman driving me to the Elysee, I was not laughed at once while in France.

LETTER VIII.

Departure from Paris--Boulogne--Folkstone--London--Geo. Thompson, Esq., M.P.--Hartwell House--Dr. Lee--Cottage of the Peasant--Windsor Castle--Residence of Wm. Penn--England's First Welcome--Heath Lodge--The Bank of England.

LONDON, **Sept. 8th**.

The sun had just appeared from behind a cloud and was setting, and its reflection upon the domes and spires of the great buildings in Paris made everything appear lovely and sublime, as the train, with almost lightning speed, was bringing me from the French metropolis. I gazed with eager eyes to catch a farewell glance of the tops of the regal palaces through which I had passed, during a stay of fifteen days in the French capital.

A pleasant ride of four hours brought us to Boulogne, where we rested for the night. The next morning I was up at an early hour, and out viewing the town. Boulogne could present but little attraction, after a fortnight spent in seeing the lions of Paris. A return to the hotel, and breakfast over, we stepped on board the steamer, and were soon crossing the channel. Two hours more, and I was safely seated in a railway carriage, *en route* to the English metropolis. We reached London at mid-day, where I was soon comfortably lodged at 22, Cecil Street, Strand. As the London lodging-houses seldom furnish dinners, I lost no time in seeking out a dining-saloon, which I had no difficulty in finding in the Strand. It being the first house of the kind I had entered in London, I was not a little annoyed at the politeness of the waiter. The first salutation I had, after seating myself in one of the stalls, was, "Ox tail, Sir; gravy soup; carrot soup, Sir; roast beef; roast pork; boiled beef; roast lamb; boiled leg of mutton, Sir, with caper sauce; jugged hare, Sir; boiled knuckle of veal and bacon; roast turkey and oyster sauce; sucking pig, Sir; curried chicken; harrico mutton, Sir." These, and many other dishes which I have forgotten, were called over with a rapidity that would have done credit to one of our Yankee pedlars, in crying his wares in a New England village. I was so completely taken by surprise, that I asked for a "bill of fare," and told him to leave me. No city in the world furnishes a cheaper, better, and quicker meal for the weary traveller, than a London eating-house.

*   *   *   *   *

After spending a day in looking about through this great thoroughfare, the Strand, I sallied forth with letters of introduction, with which I had been provided by my friends before leaving America; and following the direction of one, I was soon at No. 6, A, Waterloo Place. A moment more, and I was in the presence of one of whom I had heard much, and whose name is as familiar to the friends of the slave in the United

States, as household words. Although I had never seen him before, yet I felt a feeling akin to love for the man who had proclaimed to the oppressors of my race in America, the doctrine of ***immediate emancipation*** for the slaves of the great Republic. On reaching the door, I sent in my letter; and it being fresh from the hands of William Lloyd Garrison, the champion of freedom in the New World, was calculated to insure me a warm reception at the hands of the distinguished M.P. for the Tower Hamlets. Mr. Thompson did not wait for the servant to show me in; but met me at the door himself, and gave me a hearty shake of the hand, at the same time saying, "Welcome to England. How did you leave Garrison." I need not add, that Mr. T. gave me the best advice, as to my course in Great Britain; and how I could best serve the cause of my enslaved countrymen. I never enjoyed three hours more agreeably than those I spent with Mr. T. on the occasion of my first visit. George Thompson's love of freedom, his labours in behalf of the American slave, the negroes of the West Indies, and the wronged millions of India, are too well known to the people of both hemispheres, to need a word of comment from me. With the single exception of the illustrious Garrison, no individual is more loved and honoured by the coloured people of America, and their friends than Mr. Thompson.

A few days after my arrival in London, I received an invitation from John Lee, Esq., LL.D., whom I had met at the Peace Congress in Paris, to pay him a visit at his seat, near Aylesbury; and as the time was "fixed" by the Dr., I took the train on the appointed day, on my way to Hartwell House.

I had heard much of the aristocracy of England, and must confess that I was not a little prejudiced against them. On a bright sunshine day, between the hours of twelve and two, I found myself seated in a carriage, my back turned upon Aylesbury, the vehicle whirling rapidly over the smooth macadamised road, and I on my first visit to an English gentleman. Twenty minutes' ride, and a turn to the right, and we were amid the fine old trees of Hartwell Park; one having suspended from its branches, the national banners of several different countries; among them, the "Stars and Stripes. I felt glad that my own country's flag had a place there, although Campbell's lines"--

> "United States, your banner wears,
> Two emblems,--one of fame;
> Alas, the other that it bears,
> Reminds us of your shame.
> The white man's liberty in types,
> Stands blazoned by your stars;
> But what's the meaning of your stripes,
> They mean your Negro-scars"--

were at the time continually running through my mind. Arrived at the door, and we received what every one does who visits Dr. Lee--a hearty welcome. I was immediately shown into a room with a lofty ceiling, hung round with fine specimens of the Italian masters, and told that this was my apartment. Hartwell House stands in an extensive park, shaded with trees, that made me think of the oaks and elms in an American forest, and many of whose limbs had been trimmed and nursed with the best of care. This was for seven years the residence of John Hampden the patriot, and more recently that of Louis XVIII., during his exile in this country. The house is built on a very extensive scale, and is ornamented in the interior with carvings in wood of many of the kings and princes of bygone centuries. A room some 60 feet by 25 contains a variety of articles that the Dr. has collected together--the whole forming a museum that would be considered a sight in the Western States of America.

The morning after my arrival at Hartwell I was up at an early hour--in fact, before any of the servants--wandering about through the vast halls, and trying to find my way out, in which I eventually succeeded, but not, however, without aid. It had rained the previous night, and the sun was peeping through a misty cloud as I strolled through the park, listening to the sweet voices of the birds that were fluttering in the tops of the trees, and trimming their wings for a morning flight. The silence of the night had not yet been broken by the voice of man; and I wandered about the vast park unannoyed, except by the dew from the grass that wet my slippers. Not far from the house I came abruptly upon a beautiful little pond of water, where the gold fish were flouncing about, and the gentle ripples glittering in the sunshine looked like so many silver minnows playing on the surface.

While strolling about with pleasure, and only regretting that my dear daughters were not with me to enjoy the morning's walk, I saw the gardener on his way to the garden. I followed him, and was soon feasting my eyes upon the richest specimens of garden scenery. There were the peaches hanging upon the trees that were fastened to the wall; vegetables, fruit, and flowers were there in all their bloom and beauty; and even the variegated geranium of a warmer clime, was there in its hothouse home, and seemed to have forgotten that it was in a different country from its own. Dr. Lee shows great taste in the management of his garden. I have seldom seen a more splendid variety of fruits and flowers in the southern States of America, than I saw at Hartwell House.

I should, however, state that I was not the only guest at Hartwell during my stay. Dr. Lee had invited several others of the American delegation to the Peace Congress, and two or three of the French delegates who were on a visit to England, were enjoying the Doctor's hospitality. Dr. Lee is a staunch friend of Temperance, as well as of the cause of universal freedom. Every year he treats his tenantry to a dinner, and I need not add that these are always conducted on the principle of total abstinence.

During the second day we visited several of the cottages of the work people, and in these I took no little interest. The people of the United States know nothing of the real condition of the labouring classes of England. The peasants of Great Britain are always spoken of as belonging to the soil. I was taught in America that the English labourer was no better off than the slave upon a Carolina rice-field. I had seen the slaves in Missouri huddled together, three, four, and even five families in a single room not more than 15 by 25 feet square, and I expected to see the same in England. But in this I was disappointed. After visiting a new house that the Doctor was building, he took us into one of the cottages that stood near the road, and gave us an opportunity, of seeing, for the first time, an English peasant's cot. We entered a low whitewashed room, with a stone floor that showed an admirable degree of cleanness. Before us was a row of shelves filled with earthen dishes and pewter spoons, glittering as if they had just come from under the hand of a woman of taste. A Cobden loaf of bread, that had just been left by the baker's boy, lay upon an oaken table which had been much worn away with the scrubbing brush; while just above lay the old family bible that had been handed down from father to son, until its possession was considered of almost as great value as its contents. A half-open door, leading into another room, showed us a clean bed; the whole presenting as fine a picture of neatness, order, and comfort, as the most fastidious taste could wish to see. No occupant was present, and therefore I inspected everything with a greater degree of freedom. In front of the cottage was a small grass plot, with here and there a bed of flowers, cheated out of its share of sunshine by the tall holly that had been planted near it. As I looked upon the home of the labourer, my thoughts were with my enslaved countrymen. What a difference, thought I, there is between the tillers of the soil in England and America. There could not be a more complete refutation of the assertion that the English labourer is no better off than the American slave, than the scenes that were then before me. I called the attention of one of my American friends to a beautiful rose near the door of the cot, and said to him, "The law that will protect that flower will also guard and protect the hand that planted it." He knew that I had drank deep of the cup of slavery, was aware of what I meant, and merely nodded his head in reply. I never experienced hospitality more genuine, and yet more unpretending, than was meted out to me while at Hartwell. And the favourable impression made on my own mind, of the distinguished proprietor of Hartwell Park, was nearly as indelible as my humble name that the Doctor had engraven in a brick, in the vault beneath the Observatory in Hartwell House.

On my return to London I accepted an invitation to join a party on a visit to Windsor Castle; and taking the train at the Waterloo Bridge Station, we were soon passing through a pleasant part of the country. Arrived at the castle, we committed ourselves into the hands of the servants, and were introduced into Her Majesty's State apartments, Audience Chamber, Vandyck Room, Waterloo Chambers, St. George's Hall, Gold Pantry, and many others whose names I have forgotten. In wandering about the different apartments I lost my company, and in trying to find them, passed through a room in which hung a magnificent portrait of Charles I., by Vandyck. The hum and noise of my companions had ceased, and I had the scene and silence to myself. I looked in vain for the king's evil genius (Cromwell), but he was not in the same room. The pencil of Sir Peter Lely has left a splendid full-length likeness of James II. George IV. is suspended from a peg in the wall, looking as if it was fresh from the hands of Sir Thomas Lawrence, its admirable painter. I was now in St. George's Hall, and I gazed upward to view the beautiful figures on the ceiling, until my neck was nearly out of joint. Leaving this room, I inspected with interest the ancient **keep** of the castle. In past centuries this part of the palace was used as a prison. Here James the First of Scotland was detained a prisoner for eighteen years. I viewed the window through which the young prince had often looked to catch a glimpse of the young and beautiful Lady Jane, daughter of the Earl of Somerset, with whom he was enamoured.

From the top of the Round Tower I had a fine view of the surrounding country. Stoke Park, once the residence of that great friend of humanity and civilization, William Penn, was among the scenes that I viewed with pleasure from Windsor Castle. Four years ago, when in the city of Philadelphia, and hunting up the places associated with the name of this distinguished man, and more recently when walking over the farm once occupied by him on the banks of the Delaware, examining the old malt house which is now left standing, because of the veneration with which the name of the man who built it is held, I had no idea that I should ever see the dwelling which he had occupied in the Old World. Stoke Park is about four miles from Windsor, and is now owned by the Right Hon. Henry Labouchere.

The castle, standing as it does on an eminence, and surrounded by a beautiful valley covered with splendid villas, has the appearance of Gulliver looking down upon the Lilliputians. It rears its massive towers and irregular walls over and above every other object; it stands like a mountain in the desert. How full this old palace is of material for thought! How one could ramble here alone, or with one or two congenial companions, and enjoy a recapitulation of its history! But an engagement to be at Croydon in the evening cut short my stay at Windsor, and compelled me to return to town in advance of my party.

* * * * * *

Having met with John Morland, Esq., of Heath Lodge, at Paris, he gave me an invitation to visit Croydon, and deliver a lecture on American Slavery; and last evening, at eight o'clock, I found myself in a fine old building in the town, and facing the first English audience that I had seen in the sea-girt isle. It was my first welcome in England. The assembly was an enthusiastic one, and made still more so by the appearance of George Thompson, Esq., M.P., upon the platform. It is not my intention to give accounts of my lectures or meetings in these pages. I therefore merely say, that I left Croydon with a good impression of the English, and Heath Lodge with a feeling that its occupant was one of the most benevolent of men.

The same party with whom I visited Windsor being supplied with a card of admission to the Bank of England, I accepted an invitation to be one of the company. We entered the vast building at a little past twelve o'clock to-day. The sun threw into the large halls a brilliancy that seemed to light up the countenances of the almost countless number of clerks, who were at their desks, or serving persons at the counters. As nearly all my countrymen who visit London pay their respects to this noted institution, I shall sum up my visit to it, by saying that it surpassed my highest idea of a bank. But a stroll through this monster building of gold and silver brought to my mind an incident that occurred to me a year after my escape from slavery.

In the autumn of 1835, having been cheated out of the previous summer's earnings, by the captain of the steamer in which I had been employed running away with the money, I was, like the rest of the men, left without any means of support during the winter, and therefore had to seek employment in the neighbouring towns. I went to the town of Monroe, in the state of Michigan, and while going through the principal streets looking for work, I passed the door of the only barber in the town, whose shop appeared to be filled with persons waiting to be shaved. As there was but one man at work, and as I had, while employed in the steamer, occasionally shaved a gentleman who could not perform that office himself, it occurred to me that I might get employment here as a journeyman barber. I therefore made immediate application for work, but the barber told me he did not need a hand. But I was not to be put off so easily, and after making several offers to work cheap, I frankly told him, that if he would not employ me I would get a room near to him, and set up an opposition establishment. This threat, however, made no

impression on the barber; and as I was leaving, one of the men who were
waiting to be shaved said, "If you want a room in which to commence
business, I have one on the opposite side of the street." This man
followed me out; we went over, and I looked at the room. He strongly
urged me to set up, at the same time promising to give me his
influence. I took the room, purchased an old table, two chairs, got a
pole with a red stripe painted around it, and the next day opened, with
a sign over the door, "Fashionable Hair-dresser from New York, Emperor
of the West." I need not add that my enterprise was very annoying to the
"shop over the way"--especially my sign, which happened to be the most
expensive part of the concern. Of course, I had to tell all who came in
that my neighbour on the opposite side did not keep clean towels, that
his razors were dull, and, above all, he had never been to New York to
see the fashions. Neither had I. In a few weeks I had the entire
business of the town, to the great discomfiture of the other barber.

At this time, money matters in the Western States were in a sad
condition. Any person who could raise a small amount of money was
permitted to establish a bank, and allowed to issue notes for four times
the sum raised. This being the case, many persons borrowed money merely
long enough to exhibit to the bank inspectors, and the borrowed money
was returned, and the bank left without a dollar in its vaults, if,
indeed, it had a vault about its premises. The result was, that banks
were started all over the Western States, and the country flooded with
worthless paper. These were known as the "Wild Cat Banks." Silver coin
being very scarce, and the banks not being allowed to issue notes for a
smaller amount than one dollar, several persons put out notes from 6 to
75 cents in value; these were called "Shinplasters." The Shinplaster was
in the shape of a promissory note, made payable on demand. I have often
seen persons with large rolls of these bills, the whole not amounting to
more than five dollars. Some weeks after I had commenced business on my
"own hook," I was one evening very much crowded with customers; and
while they were talking over the events of the day, one of them said to

me, "Emperor, you seem to be doing a thriving business. You should do as other business men, issue your Shinplasters." This, of course, as it was intended, created a laugh; but with me it was no laughing matter, for from that moment I began to think seriously of becoming a banker. I accordingly went a few days after to a printer, and he, wishing to get the job of printing, urged me to put out my notes, and showed me some specimens of engravings that he had just received from Detroit. My head being already filled with the idea of a bank, I needed but little persuasion to set the thing finally afloat. Before I left the printer the notes were partly in type, and I studying how I should keep the public from counterfeiting them. The next day my Shinplasters were handed to me, the whole amount being twenty dollars, and after being duly signed were ready for circulation. At first my notes did not take well; they were too new, and viewed with a suspicious eye. But through the assistance of my customers, and a good deal of exertion on my own part, my bills were soon in circulation; and nearly all the money received in return for my notes was spent in fitting up and decorating my shop.

Few bankers get through this world without their difficulties, and I was not to be an exception. A short time after my money had been out, a party of young men, either wishing to pull down my vanity, or to try the soundness of my bank, determined to give it "a run." After collecting together a number of my bills, they came one at a time to demand other money for them, and I, not being aware of what was going on, was taken by surprise. One day as I was sitting at my table, strapping some new razors I had just got with the avails of my "Shinplasters," one of the men entered and said, "Emperor, you will oblige me if you will give me some other money for these notes of yours." I immediately cashed the notes with the most worthless of the Wild Cat money that I had on hand, but which was a lawful tender. The young man had scarcely left when a second appeared with a similar amount, and demanded payment. These were cashed, and soon a third came with his roll of notes. I paid these with an air of triumph, although I had but half a dollar left. I began now to think seriously what I should do, or how to act, provided another demand should be made. While I was thus engaged in thought, I saw the fourth man crossing the street, with a handful of notes, evidently my "Shinplasters." I instantaneously shut the door, and looking out of the window, said, "I have closed business for the day: come to-morrow and I will see you." In looking across the street, I saw my rival standing in his shop-door, grinning and clapping his hands at my apparent downfall. I was completely "done **Brown**" for the day. However, I was not to be "used up" in this way; so I escaped by the back door, and went in search of my friend who had first suggested to me the idea of issuing notes. I found him, told him of the difficulty I was in, and wished him to point out a way by which I might extricate myself. He laughed heartily, and then said, "You must act as all bankers do in this part of the country." I inquired how they did, and he said, "When your notes are brought to you, you must redeem them, and then send them out and get other money for them; and, with the latter, you can keep cashing your own Shinplasters." This was indeed a new job to me. I immediately commenced putting in circulation the notes which I had just redeemed, and my efforts were crowned with so much success, that before I slept that night my "Shinplasters" were again in circulation, and my bank once more on a sound basis.

As I saw the clerks shovelling out the yellow coin upon the counters of the Bank of England, and men coming in and going out with weighty bags of the precious metal in their hands, or on their shoulders, I could not but think of the great contrast between the monster Institution, within whose walls I was then standing, and the Wild Cat Banks of America!

LETTER IX.

The British Museum--A Portrait--Night Reading--A Dark Day--A Fugitive Slave on the Streets of London,--A Friend in the time of need.

LONDON, *Sept. 24*.

I have devoted the past ten days to sight-seeing in the Metropolis--the first two of which were spent in the British Museum. After procuring a guide-book at the door as I entered, I seated myself on the first seat that caught my eye, arranged as well as I could in my mind the different rooms, and then commenced in good earnest. The first part I visited was the Gallery of Antiquities, through to the north gallery, and thence to the Lycian Room. This place is filled with tombs, bas-reliefs, statues, and other productions of the same art. Venus, seated, and smelling a lotus flower which she held in her hand, and attended by three graces, put a stop to the rapid strides that I was making through this part of the hall. This is really one of the most precious productions of the art that I have ever seen. Many of the figures in this room are very much mutilated, yet one can linger here for hours with interest. A good number of the statues are of uncertain date; they are of great value as works of art, and more so as a means of enlightening much that has been obscure with respect to Lycia, an ancient and celebrated country of Asia Minor.

In passing through the eastern Zoological Gallery, I was surrounded on every side by an army of portraits suspended upon the walls; and among these was the Protector. The people of one century kicks his bones through the streets of London, another puts his portrait in the British Museum, and a future generation may possibly give him a place in

Westminster Abbey. Such is the uncertainty of the human character. Yesterday, a common soldier--to-day, the ruler of an empire--to-morrow, suspended upon the gallows. In an adjoining room I saw a portrait of Baxter, which gives one a pretty good idea of the great Nonconformist. In the same room hung a splendid modern portrait, without any intimation in the guide-book of who it represented, or when it was painted. It was so much like one whom I had seen, and on whom my affections were placed in my younger days, that I obtained a seat from an adjoining room and rested myself before it. After sitting half an hour or more, I wandered to another part of the building, but only to return again to my "first love," where I remained till the throng had disappeared one after another, and the officer reminding me that it was time to close.

It was eight o'clock before I reached my lodgings. Although fatigued by the day's exertions, I again resumed the reading of Roscoe's "Leo X.," and had nearly finished seventy-three pages, when the clock on St. Martin's Church apprised me that it was two. He who escapes from slavery at the age of twenty years, without any education, as did the writer of this letter, must read when others are asleep, if he would catch up with the rest of the world. "To be wise," says Pope, "is but to know how little can be known." The true searcher after truth and knowledge is always like a child; although gaining strength from year to year, he still "learns to labour and to wait." The field of labour is ever expanding before him, reminding him that he has yet more to learn; teaching him that he is nothing more than a child in knowledge, and inviting him onward with a thousand varied charms. The son may take possession of the father's goods at his death, but he cannot inherit with the property the father's cultivated mind. He may put on the father's old coat, but that is all: the immortal mind of the first wearer has gone to the tomb.

Property may be bequeathed, but knowledge cannot. Then let him who would be useful in his day and generation be up and doing. Like the

Chinese student who learned perseverance from the woman whom he saw trying to rub a crow-bar into a needle, so should we take the experience of the past to lighten our feet through the paths of the future.

The next morning at ten, I was again at the door of the great building; was soon within its walls seeing what time would not allow of the previous day. I spent some hours in looking through glass cases, viewing specimens of minerals, such as can scarcely be found in any place out of the British Museum. During this day I did not fail to visit the great Library. It is a spacious room, surrounded with large glass cases filled with volumes, whose very look tells you that they are of age. Around, under the cornice, were arranged a number of old black-looking portraits, in all probability the authors of some of the works in the glass cases beneath. About the room were placed long tables, with stands for reading and writing, and around these were a number of men busily engaged in looking over some chosen author. Old men with grey hairs, young men with mustaches--some in cloth, others in fustian, indicating that men of different rank can meet here. Not a single word was spoken during my stay, all appearing to enjoy the silence that reigned throughout the great room. This is indeed a retreat from the world. No one inquires who the man is who is at his side, and each pursues in silence his own researches. The racing of pens over the sheets of paper was all that disturbed the stillness of the occasion.

From the Library I strolled to other rooms, and feasted my eyes on what I had never before seen. He who goes over this immense building, cannot do so without a feeling of admiration for the men whose energy has brought together this vast and wonderful collection of things, the like of which cannot be found in any other museum in the world. The reflection of the setting sun against a mirror in one of the rooms, told me that night was approaching, and I had but a moment in which to take another look at the portrait that I had seen the previous day, and then bade adieu to the Museum.

Having published the narrative of my life and escape from slavery, and put it into the booksellers' hands--and seeing a prospect of a fair sale, I ventured to take from my purse the last sovereign to make up a small sum to remit to the United States, for the support of my daughter, who is at school there. Before doing this, however, I had made arrangements to attend a public meeting in the city of Worcester, at which the mayor was to preside. Being informed by the friends of the slave there, that I would, in all probability, sell a number of copies of my book, and being told that Worcester was only ten miles from London, I felt safe in parting with all but a few shillings, feeling sure that my purse would soon be again replenished. But you may guess my surprise when I learned that Worcester was above a hundred miles from London, and that I had not retained money enough to defray my expenses to the place. In my haste and wish to make up the ten pounds to send to my children, I had forgotten that the payment for my lodgings would be demanded before I should leave town. Saturday morning came; I paid my lodging bill, and had three shillings and fourpence left; and out of this sum I was to get three dinners, as I was only served with breakfast and tea at my lodgings. Nowhere in the British empire do the people witness as dark days as in London. It was on Monday morning, in the fore part of October, as the clock on St. Martin's Church was striking ten, that I left my lodgings, and turned into the Strand. The street lamps were yet burning, and the shops were all lighted as if day had not made its appearance. This great thoroughfare, as usual at this time of the day, was thronged with business men going their way, and women sauntering about for pleasure or for the want of something better to do. I passed down the Strand to Charing Cross, and looked in vain to see the majestic statue of Nelson upon the top of the great shaft. The clock on St. Martin's Church struck eleven, but my sight could not penetrate through the dark veil that hung between its face and me. In fact, day had been completely turned into night; and the brilliant lights from the shop windows almost persuaded me that another day had not appeared.

Turning, I retraced my steps, and was soon passing through the massive gates of Temple Bar, wending my way to the city, when a beggar boy at my heels accosted me for a half-penny to buy bread. I had scarcely served the boy, when I observed near by, and standing close to a lamp post, a coloured man, and from his general appearance I was satisfied that he was an American. He eyed me attentively as I passed him, and seemed anxious to speak. When I had got some distance from him I looked back, and his eyes were still upon me. No longer able to resist the temptation to speak with him, I returned, and commencing conversation with him, learned a little of his history, which was as follows. He had, he said, escaped from slavery in Maryland, and reached New York; but not feeling himself secure there, he had, through the kindness of the captain of an English ship, made his way to Liverpool; and not being able to get employment there, he had come up to London. Here he had met with no better success; and having been employed in the growing of tobacco, and being unaccustomed to any other work, he could not get to labour in England. I told him he had better try to get to the West Indies; but he informed me that he had not a single penny, and that he had nothing to eat that day. By this man's story, I was moved to tears; and going to a neighbouring shop, I took from my purse my last shilling, changed it, and gave this poor brother fugitive one-half. The poor man burst into tears as I placed the sixpence in his hand, and said--"You are the first friend I have met in London." I bade him farewell, and left him with a feeling of regret that I could not place him beyond the reach of want. I went on my way to the city, and while going through Cheapside, a streak of light appeared in the east that reminded me that it was not night. In vain I wandered from street to street, with the hope that I might meet some one who would lend me money enough to get to Worcester. Hungry and fatigued I was returning to my lodgings, when the great clock of St Paul's Church, under whose shadow I was then passing, struck four. A stroll through Fleet Street and the Strand, and I was again pacing my room. On my return, I found a letter from Worcester had arrived in my absence, informing me that a party of gentlemen would meet me the next day on my reaching that place; and saying, "Bring plenty of books, as you will doubtless sell a large number." The last sixpence had been spent for postage stamps, in order to send off some letters to other places, and I could not even stamp a letter in answer to the one last from Worcester. The only vestige of money about me was a smooth farthing that a little girl had given to me at the meeting at Croydon, saying, "This is for the slaves." I was three thousand miles from home, with but a single farthing in my pocket! Where on earth is a man without money more destitute? The cold hills of the Arctic regions have not a more inhospitable appearance than London to the stranger with an empty pocket. But whilst I felt depressed at being in such a sad condition, I was conscious that I had done right in remitting the last ten pounds to America. It was for the support of those whom God had committed to my care, and whom I love as I can no others. I had no friend in London to whom I could apply for temporary aid. My friend, Mr. Thompson, was out of town, and I did not know his address. The dark day was rapidly passing away--the clock in the hall had struck six. I had given up all hopes of reaching Worcester the next day, and had just rung the bell for the servant to bring me some tea, when a gentle tap at the door was heard--the servant entered, and informed me that a gentleman below was wishing to see me. I bade her fetch a light and ask him up. The stranger was my young friend Frederick Stevenson, son of the excellent minister of the Borough Road Chapel. I had lectured in this chapel a few days previous; and this young gentleman, with more than ordinary zeal and enthusiasm for the cause of bleeding humanity, and respect for me, had gone amongst his father's congregation and sold a number of copies of my book, and had come to bring me the money. I wiped the silent tear from my eyes as the young man placed the thirteen half-crowns in my hand. I did not let him know under what obligation I was to him for this disinterested act of kindness. He does not know to this day what aid he has rendered to a stranger in a strange land, and I feel that I am but discharging in a trifling degree, my debt of gratitude to this young gentleman, in acknowledging my obligation to him. As the man who called for bread and cheese, when feeling in his pocket for the last threepence to pay for it, found a sovereign that he was not aware he possessed, countermanded the order for the lunch, and bade them bring him the best dinner they could get; so I told the servant when she brought the tea, that I had changed my mind, and should go out to dine. With the means in my pocket of reaching Worcester the next day, I sat down to dinner at the Adelphi with a good cut of roast beef before me, and felt myself once more at home. Thus ended a dark day in London.

LETTER X.

The Whittington Club--Louis Blanc--Street Amusements--Tower of London--Westminster Abbey--National Gallery--Dante--Sir Joshua Reynolds.

LONDON, *October 10*.

For some days past, Sol has not shown his face, clouds have obscured the sky, and the rain has fallen in torrents, which has contributed much to the general gloom. However, I have spent the time in as agreeable a manner as I well could. Yesterday I fulfilled an engagement to dine with a gentleman at the Whittington Club. One who is unacquainted with the Club system as carried on in London, can scarcely imagine the conveniences they present. Every member appears to be at home, and all seem to own a share in the Club. There is a free-and-easy way with those who frequent Clubs, and a licence given there that is unknown in the drawing-room of the private mansion. I met the gentleman at the Club, at the appointed hour, and after his writing my name in the visitors' book, we proceeded to the dining-room, where we partook of a good dinner.

We had been in the room but a short time, when a small man, dressed in black, with his coat buttoned up to the chin, entered the saloon, and took a seat at the table hard by. My friend in a low whisper informed me that this person was one of the French refugees. He was apparently not more than thirty years of age, and exceedingly good looking--his person being slight, his feet and hands very small and well shaped, especially his hands, which were covered with kid gloves, so tightly drawn on, that the points of the finger nails were visible through them. His face was mild and almost womanly in its beauty, his eyes soft and full, his brow open and ample, his features well defined, and approaching to the ideal Greek in contour; the lines about his mouth were exquisitely sweet, and yet resolute in expression; his hair was short--his having no mustaches gave him nothing of the look of a Frenchman; and I was not a little surprised when informed that the person before me was Louis Blanc. I could scarcely be persuaded to believe that one so small, so child-like in stature, had taken a prominent part in the Revolution of 1848. He held in his hand a copy of *La Presse*, and as soon as he was seated, opened it and began to devour its contents. The gentleman with whom I was dining was not acquainted with him, but at the close of our dinner he procured me an introduction through another gentleman.

As we were returning to our lodgings, we saw in Exeter Street, Strand, one of those exhibitions that can be seen in almost any of the streets in the suburbs of the Metropolis, but which is something of a novelty to those from the other side of the Atlantic. This was an exhibition of "Punch and Judy." Everything was in full operation when we reached the spot. A puppet appeared eight or ten inches from the waist upwards, with an enormous face, huge nose, mouth widely grinning, projecting chin, cheeks covered with grog blossoms, a large protuberance on his back, another on his chest; yet with these deformities he appeared uncommonly happy. This was Mr. Punch. He held in his right hand a tremendous bludgeon, with which he amused himself by rapping on the head every one who came within his reach. This exhibition seems very absurd, yet not less than one hundred were present--children, boys, old men, and even gentlemen and ladies, were standing by, and occasionally greeting the performer with the smile of approbation. Mr. Punch, however, was not to have it all his own way, for another and better sort of Punch-like exhibition appeared a few yards off, that took away Mr. Punch's audience, to the great dissatisfaction of that gentleman. This was an exhibition called the Fantoccini, and far superior to any of the street performances which I have yet seen. The curtain rose and displayed a beautiful theatre in miniature, and most gorgeously painted. The organ which accompanied it struck up a hornpipe, and a sailor, dressed in his blue jacket, made his appearance and commenced keeping time with the utmost correctness. This figure was not so long as Mr. Punch, but much better looking. At the close of the hornpipe the little sailor made a bow, and tripped off, apparently conscious of having deserved the undivided applause of the bystanders. The curtain dropped; but in two or three minutes it was again up, and a rope was discovered, extended on two cross pieces, for dancing upon. The tune was changed to an air, in which the time was marked, a graceful figure appeared, jumped upon the rope with its balance pole, and displayed all the manoeuvres of an expert performer on the tight rope. Many who would turn away in disgust from Mr. Punch, will stand for hours and look at the performances of the Fantoccini. If people, like the Vicar of Wakefield, will sometimes "allow themselves to be happy," they can hardly fail to have a hearty laugh at the drolleries of the Fantoccini. There may be degrees of absurdity in the manner of wasting our time, but there is an evident affectation in decrying these humble and innocent exhibitions, by those who will sit till two or three in the morning to witness a pantomime at a theatre-royal.

* * * * *

An autumn sun shone brightly through a remarkably transparent atmosphere this morning, which was a most striking contrast to the weather we have had during the past three days; and I again set out to see some of the lions of the city, commencing with the Tower of London. Every American, on returning home from a visit to the old world, speaks with pride of the places he saw while in Europe; and of the many resorts of interest he has read of, few have made a more lasting impression upon his memory than the Tower of London. The stories of the imprisoning of kings, and queens, the murdering of princes, the torturing of men and women, without regard to birth, education, or station, and of the burning and rebuilding of the old pile, have all sunk deep into his heart. A walk of twenty minutes, after being set down at the Bank by an omnibus, brought me to the gate of the Tower. A party of friends who were to meet me there had not arrived, so I had an opportunity of inspecting the grounds and taking a good view of the external appearance of the old and celebrated building. The Tower is surrounded by a high wall, and around this a deep ditch partly filled with stagnated water. The wall incloses twelve acres of ground on which stand the several towers, occupying, with their walks and avenues, the whole space. The most ancient part of the building is called the "White Tower," so as to distinguish it from the parts more recently built. Its walls are seventeen feet in thickness, and ninety-two in height, exclusive of the turrets, of which there are four. My company arrived, and we entered the tower through four massive gates, the innermost one being pointed out as the "Water, or Traitors' Gate"--so called from the fact that it opened to the river, and through it the criminals were usually brought to the prison within. But this passage is now closed up. We visited the various apartments in the old building. The room in the Bloody Tower, where the infant princes were put to death by the command of their uncle, Richard III.; also, the recess behind the gate where the bones of the young princes were concealed, were shown to us. The warden of the prison who showed us through, seemed to have little or no veneration for Henry VIII.; for he often cracked a joke, or told a story at the expense of the murderer of Anne Boleyn. The old man wiped the tear from his eye, as he pointed out the grave of Lady Jane Grey. This was doubtless one of the best as well as most innocent of those who lost their lives in the Tower; young, virtuous, and handsome, she became a victim to the ambition of her own and her husband's relations. I tried to count the names on the wall in "Beauchamp's Tower," but they were too numerous. Anne Boleyn was imprisoned here. The room in the "Brick Tower," where Lady Jane Grey was imprisoned, was pointed out as a place of interest. We were next shown into the "White Tower." We passed through a long room filled with many things having a warlike appearance; and among them a number of equestrian figures, as large as life, and clothed in armour and trappings of the various reigns from Edward I. to James II., or from 1272 to 1685. Elizabeth, or the "Maiden Queen," as the warden called her, was the most imposing of the group; she was on a cream coloured charger. We left the Maiden Queen to examine the cloak upon which General Wolf died, at the storming of Quebec. In this room Sir Walter Raleigh was imprisoned, and here was written his "History of the World." In his own hand, upon the wall, is written, "Be thou faithful unto death, and I will give thee a crown of life." His Bible is still shown, with these memorable lines written in it by himself a short time before his death:--

> "Even such is Time that takes on trust,
> Our youth, our joy, our all we have,
> And pays us but with age and dust;
> Who in the dark and silent grave,
> When we have wandered all our ways,
> Shuts up the story of our days."

Spears, battle-axes, pikes, helmets, targets, bows and arrows, and many instruments of torture, whose names I did not learn, grace the walls of this room. The block on which the Earl of Essex and Anne Boleyn were beheaded, was shown among other objects of interest. A view of the "Queen's Jewels" closed our visit to the Tower. The Gold Staff of St. Edward, and the Baptismal Font used at the Royal christenings, made of solid silver, and more than four feet high, were among the jewels here exhibited. The Sword of Justice was there, as if to watch the rest of the valuables. However, this was not the sword that Peter used. Our acquaintance with De Foe, Sir Walter Raleigh, Chaucer, and James Montgomery, through their writings, and the knowledge that they had been incarcerated within the walls of the bastile that we were just leaving, caused us to look back again and again upon its dark grey turrets.

I closed the day with a look at the interior of St. Paul's Cathedral. A service was just over, and we met a crowd coming out as we entered the great building. "Service is over, and two pence for all that wants to stay," was the first sound that caught our ears. In the Burlesque of "Esmeralda," a man is met in the belfry of the Notre Dame at Paris, and being asked for money by one of the vergers says:--

> "I paid three pence at the door,
> And since I came in a great deal more:
> Upon my honour you have emptied my purse,
> St. Paul's Cathedral could not do worse."

I felt inclined to join in this sentiment before I left the church. A fine statue of "Surly Sam" Johnson was one of the first things that caught our eyes on looking around. A statue of Sir Edward Packenham, who fell at the Battle of New Orleans, was on the opposite side of the great hall. As we had walked over the ground where this General fell, we viewed his statue with more than ordinary interest. We were taken from one scene of interest to another, until we found ourselves in the "Whispering Gallery." From the dome we had a splendid view of the

Metropolis of the world. A scaffold was erected up here to enable an artist to take sketches from which a panorama of London was painted. The artist was three years at work. The painting is now exhibited at the Colosseum; but the brain of the artist was turned, and he died insane! Indeed, one can scarcely conceive how it could be otherwise. You in America have no idea of the immensity of this building. Pile together half-a-dozen of the largest churches in New York or Boston, and you will have but a faint representation of St. Paul's Cathedral.

*   *   *   *   *

I have just returned from a stroll of two hours through Westminster Abbey. We entered the building at a door near Poets' Corner, and, naturally enough, looked around for the monuments of the men whose imaginative powers have contributed so much to instruct and amuse mankind. I was not a little disappointed in the few I saw. In almost any church-yard you may see monuments and tombs far superior to anything in the Poets' Corner. A few only have monuments. Shakspere, who wrote of man to man, and for man to the end of time, is honoured with one. Addison's monument is also there; but the greater number have nothing more erected to their memories than busts or medallions. Poets' Corner is not splendid in appearance, yet I observed visitors lingering about it, as if they were tied to the spot by love and veneration for some departed friend. All seemed to regard it as classic ground. No sound louder than a whisper was heard during the whole time, except the verger treading over the marble floor with a light step. There is great pleasure in sauntering about the tombs of those with whom we are familiar through their writings; and we tear ourselves from their ashes, as we would from those of a bosom friend. The genius of these men spreads itself over the whole panorama of Nature, giving us one vast and varied picture, the colour of which will endure to the end of time. None can portray like the poet the passions of the human soul. The statue of Addison, clad in his dressing-gown, is not far from that of Shakspere.

He looks as if he had just left the study, after finishing some chosen paper for the ***Spectator***. This memento of a great man, was the work of the British public. Such a mark of national respect was but justice to one who has contributed more to purify and raise the standard of English literature, than any man of his day. We next visited the other end of the same transept, near the northern door. Here lie Mansfield, Chatham, Fox, the second William Pitt, Grattan, Wilberforce, and a few other statesmen. But, above all, is the stately monument to the Earl of Chatham. In no other place so small, do so many great men lie together. To these men, whose graves strangers from all parts of the world wish to view, the British public are in a great measure indebted for England's fame. The high pre-eminence which England has so long enjoyed and maintained in the scale of empire, has constantly been the boast and pride of the English people. The warm panegyrics that have been lavished on her constitution and laws--the songs chaunted to celebrate her glory--the lustre of her arms, as the glowing theme of her warriors--the thunder of her artillery in proclaiming her moral prowess, her flag being unfurled to every breeze and ocean, rolling to her shores the tribute of a thousand realms--show England to be the greatest nation in the world, and speak volumes for the great departed, as well as for those of the living present. One requires no company, no amusements, no books in such a place as this. Time and death have placed within those walls sufficient to occupy the mind, if one should stay here a week.

On my return, I spent an hour very pleasantly in the National Academy, in the same building as the National Gallery. Many of the paintings here are of a fine order. Oliver Cromwell looking upon the headless corpse of King Charles I., appeared to draw the greatest number of spectators. A scene from "As You Like it," was one of the best executed pieces we saw. This was "Rosalind, Celia, and Orlando." The artist did himself and the subject great credit. Kemble, in Hamlet, with that ever memorable skull in his hand, was one of the pieces which we viewed with no little interest. It is strange that Hamlet is always represented as a thin, lean man, when the Hamlet of Shakspere was a fat, John Bull-kind of a man. But the best piece in the Gallery was "Dante meditating the episode of Francesca da Rimini and Paolo Malatesta, S'Inferno, Canto V." Our first interest for the great Italian poet was created by reading Lord Byron's poem, "The Lament of Dante." From that hour we felt like examining everything connected with the great Italian poet. The history of poets, as well as painters, is written in their works. The best written life of Goldsmith is to be found in his poem of "The Traveller," and his novel of "The Vicar of Wakefield." Boswell could not have written a better life of himself than he has done in giving the Biography of Dr. Johnson. It seems clear that no one can be a great poet without having been sometime during life a lover, and having lost the object of his affection in some mysterious way. Burns had his Highland Mary, Byron his Mary, and Dante was not without his Beatrice. Whether there ever lived such a person as Beatrice seems to be a question upon which neither of his biographers have thrown much light. However, a Beatrice existed in the poet's mind, if not on earth. His attachment to Beatrice Portinari, and the linking of her name with the immortality of his great poem, left an indelible impression upon his future character. The marriage of the object of his affections to another, and her subsequent death, and the poet's exile from his beloved Florence, together with his death amongst strangers--all give an interest to the poet's writings, which could not be heightened by romance itself. When exiled and in poverty, Dante found a friend in the father of Francesca. And here, under the roof of his protector, he wrote his great poem. The time the painter has chosen is evening. Day and night meet in mid-air: one star is alone visible. Sailing in vacancy are the shadows of the lovers. The countenance of Francesca is expressive of hopeless agony. The delineations are sublime, the conception is of the highest order, and the execution admirable. Dante is seated in a marble vestibule, in a meditating attitude, the face partly concealed by the right hand upon which it is resting. On the whole, it is an excellently painted piece, and causes one to go back with a fresh relish to the Italian's celebrated poem. In coming out, we stopped a short while in the upper room of the Gallery, and spent a few minutes over a painting representing Mrs. Siddons in one of Shakspere's characters. This is by Sir Joshua Reynolds, and is only one of the many pieces that we have seen of this great artist. His genius was vast, and powerful in its grasp. His fancy fertile, and his inventive faculty inexhaustible in its resources. He displayed the very highest powers of genius by the thorough originality of his conceptions, and by the entirely new path that he struck out in art. Well may Englishmen be proud of his name. And as time shall step between his day and those that follow after him, the more will his works be appreciated. We have since visited his grave, and stood over his monument in St. Paul's.

LETTER XI.

York Minster--The Great Organ--Newcastle-on-Tyne--The Labouring Classes--The American Slave--Sheffield--James Montgomery.

January, 1850.

Some days since, I left the Metropolis to fulfil a few engagements to visit provincial towns; and after a ride of nearly eight hours, we were in sight of the ancient city of York. It was night, the moon was in her zenith, and there seemed nothing between her and the earth but glittering gold. The moon, the stars, and the innumerable gas-lights, gave the city a panoramic appearance. Like a mountain starting out of a plain, there stood the Cathedral in all its glory, looking down upon the surrounding buildings, with all the appearance of a Gulliver standing over the Lilliputians. Night gave us no opportunity to view the

Minster. However, we were up the next morning before the sun, and walking round the Cathedral with a degree of curiosity seldom excited within us. It is thought that a building of the same dimensions would take fifty years to complete it at the present time, even with all the improvements of the nineteenth century, and would cost no less than the enormous sum of two millions of pounds sterling. From what I had heard of this famous Cathedral, my expectations were raised to the highest point; but it surpassed all the idea that I had formed of it. On entering the building, we lost all thought of the external appearance by the matchless beauty of the interior. The echo produced by the tread of our feet upon the floor as we entered, resounding through the aisles, seemed to say "Put off your shoes, for the place whereon you tread is holy ground." We stood with hat in hand, and gazed with wonder and astonishment down the incomparable vista of more than five hundred feet. The organ, which stands near the centre of the building, is said to be one of the finest in the world. A wall, in front of which is a screen of the most gorgeous and florid architecture and executed in solid stone, separates the nave from the service choir. The beautiful workmanship of this makes it appear so perfect, as almost to produce the belief that it is tracery work of wood. We ascended the rough stone steps through a winding stair to the turrets, where we had such a view of the surrounding country, as can be obtained from no other place. On the top of the centre and highest turret, is a grotesque figure of a fiddler; rather a strange looking object, we thought, to occupy the most elevated pinnacle on the house of God. All dwellings in the neighbourhood appear like so many dwarfs couching at the feet of the Minster; while its own vastness and beauty impress the observer with feelings of awe and sublimity. As we stood upon the top of this stupendous mountain of ecclesiastical architecture, and surveyed the picturesque hills and valleys around, imagination recalled the tumult of the sanguinary battles fought in sight of the edifice. The rebellion of Octavius near three thousand years ago, his defeat and flight to the Scots, his return and triumph over the Romans, and being crowned king of all Britain; the assassination of Oswald king of the Northumbrians; the flaying alive of Osbert; the crowning of Richard III; the siege by William the Conqueror; the siege by Cromwell, and the pomp and splendour with which the different monarchs had been received in York, all appeared to be vividly before me. While we were thus calling to our aid our knowledge of history, a sweet peal from the lungs of the ponderous organ below cut short our stay among the turrets, and we descended to have our organ of tune gratified, as well as to finish the inspection of the interior.

I have heard the sublime melodies of Handel, Hayden, and Mozart, performed by the most skilful musicians; I have listened with delight and awe to the soul-moving compositions of those masters, as they have been chaunted in the most magnificent churches; but never did I hear such music, and played upon such an instrument, as that sent forth by the great organ in the Cathedral of York. The verger took much delight in showing us the Horn that was once mounted with gold, but is now garnished with brass. We viewed the monuments and tombs of the departed, and then spent an hour before the great north window. The designs on the painted glass, which tradition states was given to the church by five virgin sisters, is the finest thing of the kind in Great Britain. I felt a relief on once more coming into the open air and again beholding Nature's own sun-light. The splendid ruins of St. Mary's Abbey, with its eight beautiful light gothic windows, next attracted our attention. A visit to the Castle finished our stay in York; and as we were leaving the old city we almost imagined that we heard the chiming of the bells for the celebration of the first Christian Sabbath, with Prince Arthur as the presiding genius.

*   *   *   *   *

England stands pre-eminently the first government in the world for freedom of speech and of the press. Not even in our own beloved America, can the man who feels himself oppressed speak as he can in Great Britain. In some parts of England, however, the freedom of thought is tolerated to a greater extent than in others; and of the places favourable to reforms of all kinds, calculated to elevate and benefit mankind, Newcastle-on-Tyne doubtless takes the lead. Surrounded by innumerable coal mines, it furnishes employment for a large labouring population, many of whom take a deep interest in the passing events of the day, and, consequently, are a reading class. The public debater or speaker, no matter what may be his subject, who fails to get an audience in other towns, is sure of a gathering in the Music Hall, or Lecture Room in Newcastle. Here I first had an opportunity of coming in contact with a portion of the labouring people of Britain. I have addressed large and influential meetings in Newcastle and the neighbouring towns, and the more I see and learn of the condition of the working-classes of England the more I am satisfied of the utter fallacy of the statements often made that their condition approximates to that of the slaves of America. Whatever may be the disadvantages that the British peasant labours under, he is free; and if he is not satisfied with his employer he can make choice of another. He also has the right to educate his children; and he is the equal of the most wealthy person before an English Court of Justice. But how is it with the American Slave? He has no right to himself, no right to protect his wife, his child, or his own person. He is nothing more than a living tool. Beyond his field or workshop he knows nothing. There is no amount of ignorance he is not capable of. He has not the least idea of the face of this earth, nor of the history or constitution of the country in which he dwells. To him the literature, science, and art--the progressive history, and the accumulated discoveries of bygone ages, are as if they had never been. The past is to him as yesterday, and the future scarcely more than to-morrow. Ancestral monuments, he has none; written documents fraught with cogitations of other times, he has none; and any instrumentality calculated to awaken and expound the intellectual activity and comprehension of a present or approaching generation, he has none. His condition is that of the leopard of his own native Africa. It lives, it propagates its kind; but never does it indicate a movement towards that all but angelic intelligence of man. The slave eats, drinks, and sleeps--all for the benefit of the man who claims his body as his property. Before the tribunals of his country he has no voice. He has no higher appeal than the mere will of his owner. He knows nothing of the inspired Apostles through their writings. He has no Sabbath, no Church, no Bible, no means of grace,--and yet we are told that he is as well off as the labouring classes of England. It is not enough that the people of my country should point to their Declaration of Independence which declares that "all men are created equal." It is not enough that they should laud to the skies a constitution containing boasting declarations in favour of freedom. It is not enough that they should extol the genius of Washington, the patriotism of Henry, or the enthusiasm of Otis. The time has come when nations are judged by the acts of the present instead of the past. And so it must be with America. In no place in the United Kingdom has the American Slave warmer friends than in Newcastle.

* * * * *

I am now in Sheffield, and have just returned from a visit to James Montgomery, the poet. In company with James Wall, Esq., I proceeded to The Mount, the residence of Mr. Montgomery; and our names being sent in, we were soon in the presence of the "Christian Poet." He held in his left hand the **Eclectic Review** for the month, and with the right gave me a hearty shake, and bade me "Welcome to old England." He was anything but like the portraits I had seen of him, and the man I had in my mind's eye. I had just been reading his "Pelican Island," and I eyed the poet with no little interest. He is under the middle size, his forehead high and well formed, the top of which was a little bald; his hair of a yellowish colour, his eyes rather small and deep set, the nose long and slightly aquiline, his mouth rather small, and not at all pretty. He was dressed in black, and a large white cravat entirely hid his neck and chin: his having been afflicted from childhood with salt-rhum, was doubtless the cause of his chin being so completely buried in the neckcloth. Upon the whole, he looked more like one of our American Methodist parsons, than any one I have seen in this country. He entered freely into conversation with us. He said he should be glad to attend my lecture that evening, but that he had long since quit going out at night. He mentioned having heard William Lloyd Garrison some years before, and with whom he was well pleased. He said it had long been a puzzle to him, how Americans could hold slaves and still retain their membership in the churches. When we rose to leave, the old man took my hand between his two, and with tears in his eyes said, "Go on your Christian mission, and may the Lord protect and prosper you. Your enslaved countrymen have my sympathy, and shall have my prayers." Thus ended our visit to the Bard of Sheffield. Long after I had quitted the presence of the poet, the following lines of his were ringing in my ears:--

> "Wanderer, whither dost thou roam?
> Weary wanderer, old and grey,
> Wherefore has thou left thine home,
> In the sunset of thy day.
> Welcome wanderer as thou art,
> All my blessings to partake;
> Yet thrice welcome to my heart,
> For thine injured people's sake.
> Wanderer, whither would'st thou roam?
> To what region far away?
> Bend thy steps to find a home,
> In the twilight of thy day.
> Where a tyrant never trod,
> Where a slave was never known--
> But where Nature worships God
> In the wilderness alone."

Mr. Montgomery seems to have thrown his entire soul into his meditations on the wrongs of Switzerland. The poem from which we have just quoted, is unquestionably one of his best productions, and contains more of the fire of enthusiasm than all his other works. We feel a reverence almost amounting to superstition, for the poet who deals with nature. And who is more capable of understanding the human heart than the poet? Who has better known the human feelings than Shakspere; better painted than Milton, the grandeur of Virtue; better sighed than Byron over the subtle weaknesses of Hope? Who ever had a sounder taste, a more exact intellect than Dante? or who has ever tuned his harp more in favour of Freedom, than our own Whittier?

LETTER XII.

Kirkstall Abbey--Mary the Maid of the Inn--Newstead Abbey: Residence of Lord Byron--Parish Church of Hucknall--Burial Place of Lord Byron--Bristol: "Cook's Folly"--Chepstow Castle and Abbey--Tintern Abbey--Redcliffe Church.

January 29.

In passing through Yorkshire, we could not resist the temptation it offered, to pay a visit to the extensive and interesting ruin of Kirkstall Abbey, which lies embosomed in a beautiful recess of Airedale, about three miles from Leeds. A pleasant drive over a smooth road, brought us abruptly in sight of the Abbey. The tranquil and pensive beauty of the desolate Monastery, as it reposes in the lap of pastoral luxuriance, and amidst the touching associations of seven centuries, is almost beyond description when viewed from where we first beheld it. After arriving at its base, we stood for some moments under the mighty arches that lead into the great hall, gazing at its old grey walls frowning with age. At the distance of a small field, the Aire is seen gliding past the foot of the lawn on which the ruin stands, after it has left those precincts, sparkling over a weir with a pleasing murmur. We could fully enter into the feelings of the Poet when he says:--

> "Beautiful fabric! even in decay
> And desolation, beauty still is thine;
> As the rich sunset of an autumn day,
> When gorgeous clouds in glorious hues combine
> To render homage to its slow decline,
> Is more majestic in its parting hour:
> Even so thy mouldering, venerable shrine
> Possesses now a more subduing power,
> Than in thine earlier sway, with pomp and pride thy dower."

The tale of "Mary, the Maid of the Inn," is supposed, and not without foundation, to be connected with this Abbey. "Hark to Rover," the name of the house where the key is kept, was, a century ago, a retired inn or pot-house, and the haunt of many a desperate highwayman and poacher. The anecdote is so well known, that it is scarcely necessary to relate it. It, however, is briefly this:--

"One stormy night, as two travellers sat at the inn, each having exhausted his news, the conversation was directed to the Abbey, the boisterous night, and Mary's heroism; when a bet was at last made by one of them, that she would not go and bring back from the nave a slip of the alder-tree growing there. Mary, however, did go; but having nearly reached the tree, she heard a low, indistinct dialogue; at the same time, something black fell and rolled towards her, which afterwards proved to be a hat. Directing her attention to the place whence the conversation proceeded, she saw, from behind a pillar, two men carrying a murdered body: they passed near the place where she stood, a heavy cloud was swept from off the face of the moon, and Mary fell senseless--one of the murderers was her intended husband! She was awakened from her swoon, but--her reason had fled for ever." Mr. Southey wrote a beautiful poem founded on this story, which will be found in his published works. We spent nearly three hours in wandering through these splendid ruins. It is both curious and interesting to trace the early history of these old piles, which become the resort of thousands, nine-tenths of whom are unaware either of the classic ground on which they tread, or of the peculiar interest thrown around the spot by the deeds of remote ages.

During our stay in Leeds, we had the good fortune to become acquainted with Wilson Armistead, Esq. This gentleman is well known as an able writer against Slavery. His most elaborate work is "A Tribute for the Negro." This is a volume of 560 pages, and is replete with facts refuting the charges of inferiority brought against the Negro race. Few English gentlemen have done more to hasten the day of the American slave's liberation, than Wilson Armistead.

*   *   *   *   *

We have just paid a visit to Newstead Abbey, the far-famed residence of Lord Byron. I posted from Hucknall over to Newstead one pleasant morning, and, being provided with a letter of introduction to Colonel Wildman, I lost no time in presenting myself at the door of the Abbey. But, unfortunately for me, the Colonel was at Mansfield, in attendance at the Assizes--he being one of the County Magistrates. I did not however lose the object of my visit, as every attention was paid in showing me about the premises. I felt as every one must, who gazes for the first time upon these walls, and remembers that it was here, even amid the comparative ruins of a building once dedicated to the sacred cause of Religion and her twin sister, Charity, that the genius of Byron was first developed. Here that he paced with youthful melancholy the halls of his illustrious ancestors, and trode the walks of the long-banished monks. The housekeeper--a remarkably good looking and polite woman--showed us through the different apartments, and explained in the most minute manner every object of interest connected with the interior of the building. We first visited the Monks' Parlour, which seemed to contain nothing of note, except a very fine stained window--one of the figures representing St. Paul, surmounted by a cross. We passed through Lord Byron's Bedroom, the Haunted Chamber, the Library, and the Eastern Corridor, and halted in the Tapestry Bedroom, which is truly a magnificent apartment, formed by the Byrons for the use of King Charles II. The ceiling is richly decorated with the Byron arms. We next visited the grand Drawing-room, probably the finest in the building. This saloon contains a large number of splendid portraits, among which is the celebrated portrait of Lord Byron, by Phillips. In this room we took into our hand the Skull-cup, of which so much has been written, and that has on it a short inscription, commencing with--"Start not--nor deem my spirit fled." Leaving this noble room, we descended by a few polished oak steps into the West Corridor, from which we entered the grand Dining Hall, and through several other rooms, until we reached the Chapel. Here we were shown a stone coffin which had been found near the high altar, when the workmen were excavating the vault, intended by Lord Byron for himself and his dog. The coffin contained the skeleton of an Abbot, and also the identical skull from which the cup, of which I have made mention, was made. We then left the building, and took a stroll through the grounds. After passing a pond of cold crystal water, we came to a dark wood in which are two leaden statues of Pan, and a female satyr--very fine specimens as works of art. We here inspected the tree whereon Byron carved his own name and that of his sister, with the date, all of which are still legible. However, the tree is now dead, and we were informed that Colonel Wildman intended to have it cut down so as to preserve the part containing the inscription. After crossing an interesting and picturesque part of the gardens, we arrived within the precincts of the ancient Chapel, near which we observed a neat marble monument, and which we supposed to have been erected to the memory of some of the Byrons; but, on drawing near to it, we read the following inscription:--

> "Near this spot
> are deposited the remains of one
> who possessed beauty without vanity,
> strength without insolence,
> courage without ferocity,
> and all the virtues of man without his vices.
> This praise, which would be unmeaning flattery,
> if inscribed over human ashes,
> is but a just tribute to the memory of
> BOATSWAIN, a dog,
> Who was born at Newfoundland, May, 1803,
> and died at Newstead Abbey, November 18, 1808."

By a will which his Lordship executed in 1811, he directed that his own body should be buried in a vault in the garden, near his faithful dog. This feeling of affection to his dumb and faithful follower, commendable in itself, seems here to have been carried beyond the bounds of reason and propriety.

In another part of the grounds we saw the oak tree planted by the poet himself. It has now attained a goodly size, considering the growth of the oak, and bids fair to become a lasting memento to the Noble Bard, and to be a shrine to which thousands of pilgrims will resort in future ages, to do homage to his mighty genius. This tree promises to share in after times the celebrity of Shakspere's mulberry, and Pope's willow. Near by, and in the tall trees, the rooks were keeping up a tremendous noise. After seeing everything of interest connected with the great poet, we entered our chaise, and left the premises. As we were leaving, I turned to take a farewell look at the Abbey, standing in solemn grandeur, the long ivy clinging fondly to the rich tracery of a former age. Proceeding to the little town of Hucknall, we entered the old grey Parish Church, which has for ages been the last resting-place of the Byrons, and where repose the ashes of the Poet, marked only by a neat marble slab, bearing the date of the poet's birth, death, and the fact that the tablet was placed there by his sister. This closed my visit to the interesting scenes associated with Byron's strange eventful history--scenes that ever acquire a growing charm as the lapse of years softens the errors of the man, and confirms the genius of the poet.

* * * * *

May 10.

It was on a lovely morning that I found myself on board the little steamer *Wye*, passing out of Bristol harbour. In going down the river, we saw on our right, the stupendous rocks of St. Vincent towering some four or five hundred feet above our heads. By the swiftness of our fairy steamer, we were soon abreast of Cook's Folly, a singular tower, built by a man from whom it takes its name, and of which the following romantic story is told:--"Some years since a gentleman, of the name of Cook, erected this tower, which has since gone by the name of 'Cook's Folly.' A son having been born, he was desirous of ascertaining, by means of astrology, if he would live to enjoy his property. Being himself a firm believer, like the poet Dryden, that certain information might be obtained from the above science, he caused the child's horoscope to be drawn, and found, to his dismay, that in his third, sixteenth, or twenty-first year, he would be in danger of meeting with some fearful calamity or sudden death, to avert which he caused the turret to be constructed, and the child placed therein. Secure, as he vainly thought, there he lived, attended by a faithful servant, their food and fuel being conveyed to them by means of a pully-basket, until he was old enough to wait upon himself. On the eve of his twenty-first year, his parent's hopes rose high, and great were the rejoicings prepared to welcome the young heir to his home. But, alas! no human skill could avert the dark fate which clung to him. The last night he had to pass alone in the turret, a bundle of faggots was conveyed to him as usual, in which lay concealed a viper, which clung to his hand. The bite was fatal; and, instead of being borne in triumph, the dead body of his only son was the sad spectacle which met the sight of his father."

We crossed the channel and soon entered the mouth of that most picturesque of rivers, the Wye. As we neared the town of Chepstow the old Castle made its appearance, and a fine old ruin it is. Being previously provided with a letter of introduction to a gentleman in Chepstow, I lost no time in finding him out. This gentleman gave me a cordial reception, and did what Englishmen seldom ever do, lent me his saddle horse to ride to the Abbey. While lunch was in preparation I took a stroll through the Castle which stood near by. We entered the Castle through the great door-way and were soon treading the walls that had once sustained the cannon and the sentinel, but were now covered with weeds and wild flowers. The drum and fife had once been heard within these walls--the only music now is the cawing of the rook and daw. We paid a hasty visit to the various apartments, remaining longest in those of most interest. The room in which Martin the Regicide was imprisoned nearly twenty years, was pointed out to us. The Castle of Chepstow is still a magnificent pile, towering upon the brink of a stupendous cliff, on reaching the top of which, we had a splendid view of the surrounding country. Time, however, compelled us to retrace our steps, and after partaking of a lunch, we mounted a horse for the first time in ten years, and started for Tintern Abbey. The distance from Chepstow to the Abbey is about five miles, and the road lies along the banks of the river. The river is walled in on either side by hills of much beauty, clothed from base to summit with the richest verdure. I can conceive of nothing more striking than the first appearance of the Abbey. As we rounded a hill, all at once we saw the old ruin standing before us in all its splendour. This celebrated ecclesiastical relic of the olden time is doubtless the finest ruin of its kind in Europe. Embosomed amongst hills, and situated on the banks of the most fairy-like river in the world, its beauty can scarcely be surpassed. We halted at the "Beaufort Arms," left our horse, and sallied forth to view the Abbey. The sun was pouring a flood of light upon the old grey walls, lighting up its dark recesses, as if to give us a better opportunity of viewing it. I gazed with astonishment and admiration at its many beauties, and especially at the superb gothic windows over the entrance door. The beautiful gothic pillars, with here and there a representation of a praying priest, and mailed knights, with saints and Christian martyrs, and the hundreds of Scriptural representations, all indicate that this was a place of considerable importance in its palmy days. The once stone floor had disappeared, and we found ourselves standing on a floor of unbroken green grass, swelling back to the old walls, and looking so verdant and silken that it seemed the very floor of fancy. There are more romantic and wilder places than this in the world, but none more beautiful. The preservation of these old abbeys should claim the attention of those under whose charge they are, and we felt like joining with the poet and saying:--

> "O ye who dwell
> Around yon ruins, guard the precious charge
> From hands profane! O save the sacred pile--
> O'er which the wing of centuries has flown
> Darkly and silently, deep-shadowing all

> Its pristine honours--from the ruthless grasp
> Of future violation."

In contemplating these ruins more closely, the mind insensibly reverts to the period of feudal and regal oppression, when structures like that of Tintern Abbey necessarily became the scenes of stirring and highly-important events. How altered is the scene! Where were formerly magnificence and splendour; the glittering array of priestly prowess; the crowded halls of haughty bigots, and the prison of religious offenders; there is now but a heap of mouldering ruins. The oppressed and the oppressor have long since lain down together in the peaceful grave. The ruin, generally speaking, is unusually perfect, and the sculpture still beautifully sharp. The outward walls are nearly entire, and are thickly clad with ivy. Many of the windows are also in a good state of preservation; but the roof has long since fallen in. The feathered songsters were fluttering about, and pouring forth their artless lays as a tribute of joy; while the lowing of the herds, the bleating of flocks, and the hum of bees upon the farm near by, all burst upon the ear, and gave the scene a picturesque sublimity that can be easier imagined than described. Most assuredly Shakspere had such ruins in view when he exclaimed--

> "The cloud-capp'd towers, the gorgeous palaces,
> The solemn temples, the great globe itself,
> Yea, all which it inherit, shall dissolve--
> And, like the baseless fabric of a vision,
> Leave not a wreck behind."

In the afternoon we returned to Bristol, and I spent the greater part of the next day in examining the interior of Redcliffe Church. Few places in the West of England have greater claims upon the topographer and historian than the church of St. Mary's, Redcliffe. Its antiquity, the beauty of its architecture, and above all the interesting circumstances connected with its history, entitle it to peculiar notice. It is also associated with the enterprise of genius; for its name has been blended with the reputation of Rowley, of Canynge, and of Chatterton; and no lover of poetry and admirer of art can visit it without a degree of enthusiasm. And when the old building shall have mouldered into ruins, even these will be trodden with veneration as sacred to the recollection of genius of the highest order. Ascending a winding stair, we were shown into the Treasury Room. The room forms an irregular octagon, admitting light through narrow unglazed apertures upon the broken and scattered fragments of the famous Rowleian chests, that with the rubble and dust of centuries cover the floor. It is here creative fancy pictures forth the sad image of the spirit of the spot--the ardent boy, flushed and fed by hope, musing on the brilliant deception he had conceived--whose daring attempt has left his name unto the intellectual world as a marvel and a mystery.

That a boy under twelve years of age should write a series of poems, imitating the style of the fifteenth century, and palm these poems off upon the world as the work of a monk, is indeed strange; and that these should become the object of interesting contemplation to the literary world, and should awaken inquiries, and exercise the talents of a Southey, a Bryant, a Miller, a Mathias, and others, savours more of romance than reality. I had visited the room in a garret in High Holborn, where this poor boy died. I had stood over a grave in the burial-ground of the Lane Workhouse, which was pointed out to me as the last resting-place of Chatterton; and now I was in the room where it was alleged he obtained the manuscripts that gave him such notoriety. We descended and viewed other portions of the church. The effect of the chancel, as seen behind the pictures, is very singular, and suggestive of many swelling thoughts. We look at the great east window, it is unadorned with its wonted painted glass; we look at the altar-screen beneath, on which the light of day again falls, and behold the injuries it has received at the hands of time. There is a dreary mournfulness in the scene which fastens on the mind, and is in unison with the time-worn mouldering fragments that are seen all around us. And this dreariness is not removed by our tracing the destiny of man on the storied pavements or on the graven brass, that still bears upon its surface the names of those who obtained the world's regard years back. This old pile is not only an ornament to the city, but it stands a living monument to the genius of its founder. Bristol has long sustained a high position as a place from which the American Abolitionists have received substantial encouragement in their arduous labours for the emancipation of the slaves of that land; and the writer of this received the best evidence that in this respect the character of the people had not been exaggerated, especially as regards the "Clifton Ladies' Anti-Slavery Society."

LETTER XXIII[1].

Aberdeen--Passage by Steamer--Edinburgh--Visit to the College--William and Ellen Craft.

I have visited few places where I found more warm friends than in Aberdeen. This is the Granite City of Scotland.

Aberdeen reminds one of Boston, especially in a walk down Union Street,

---

1 This letter is rather out of its proper place here. I had mislaid the MS., and my distance from the printer prevented the matter being rectified. In another edition, the transposition can be effected.

which is said to be one of the finest promenades in Europe.

The town is situated on a neck of land between the rivers Dee and Don, and is the most important place in the north of Scotland. During our third day in the city, we visited among other places the Old Bridge of Don, which is not only resorted to on account of its antique celebrity and peculiar appearance, but also because of the notoriety that it has gained by Lord Byron's poem of the "Bridge of Don."

An engagement to be in Edinburgh and vicinity, cut short our stay in the north. The very mild state of the weather, and a wish to see something of the coast between Aberdeen and Edinburgh, induced us to make the journey by water.

On Friday evening, the 14th, after delivering a lecture before the Total Abstinence Society, in company with William and Ellen Craft, I went on board the steamer bound for Edinburgh. On reaching the vessel, we found the drawing-room almost entirely at our service, and prejudice against colour being unknown, we had no difficulty in getting the best accommodation which the steamer could furnish. This is so unlike the pro-slavery, negro-hating spirit of America, that the Crafts seemed almost bewildered by the transition. I had been in the saloon but a short time, when, looking at the newspapers on the table, I discovered the ***North Star***. It was like meeting with a friend in a strange land. I looked in vain on the margin for the name of its owner, but as I did not feel at liberty to take it, and as it appeared to be alone, I laid the ***Liberator*** by its side to keep it company.

The night was a glorious one. The sky was without a speck; and the clear, piercing air had a brilliancy I have seldom seen. The moon was in its zenith--the steamer and surrounding objects were beautiful in the extreme. The boat got under weigh at a little past twelve, and we were soon out at sea. The "Queen" is a splendid craft, and without the aid of sails, was able to make fifteen miles within the hour. I was up the next morning before the sun, and found the sea as on the previous night--as calm and smooth as a mirror. It was a delightful morning, more like April than February; and the sun, as it rose, seemed to fire every peak of the surrounding hills. On our left, lay the Island of May, while to the right was to be seen the small fishing town of Anstruther, twenty miles distant from Edinburgh. Beyond these, on either side, was a range of undulating blue mountains, swelling as they retired, into a bolder outline and a loftier altitude, until they terminated some twenty-five or thirty miles in the dim distance. A friend at my side pointed out a place on the right, where the remains of an old castle or look-out house, used in the time of the border wars, once stood, and which reminded us of the barbarism of the past.

But these signs are fast disappearing. The plough and roller have passed over many of these foundations, and the time will soon come, when the antiquarian will look in vain for those places that history has pointed out to him, as connected with the political and religious struggles of the past. The steward of the vessel came round to see who of the passengers wished for breakfast, and as the keen air of the morning had given me an appetite, and there being no prejudice on the score of colour, I took my seat at the table and gave ample evidence that I was not an invalid. On returning to the deck again, I found we had entered the Forth, and that "Modern Athens" was in sight; and, far above every other object, with its turrets almost lost in the clouds, could be seen Edinburgh Castle. After landing, a pleasant ride over one of the finest roads in Scotland, with a sprinkling of beautiful villas on either side, brought us once more to Cannon's Hotel.

In a city like Edinburgh, there is always something to keep the public alive, but during our three days' stay in the town, on this occasion, there were topics under discussion which seemed to excite the people, although I had been told that the Scotch were not excitable. Indeed all

Edinburgh seemed to have gone mad about the Pope. If his Holiness should think fit to pay a visit to his new dominions, I would advise him to keep out of reach of the Scotch.

In company with the Crafts, I visited the Calton Hill, from which we had a delightful view of the city and surrounding country. I had an opportunity during my stay in the city, of visiting the Infirmary, and was pleased to see among the two or three hundred students, three coloured young men, seated upon the same benches with those of a fairer complexion, and yet there appeared no feeling on the part of the whites towards their coloured associates, except of companionship and respect. One of the cardinal truths, both of religion and freedom, is the equality and brotherhood of man. In the sight of God and all just institutions, the whites can claim no precedence or privilege, on account of their being white; and if coloured men are not treated as they should be in the educational institutions in America, it is a pleasure to know that all distinction ceases by crossing the broad Atlantic. I had scarcely left the lecture room of the Institute and reached the street, when I met a large number of the students on their way to the college, and here again were seen coloured men arm in arm with whites. The proud American who finds himself in the splendid streets of Edinburgh, and witnesses such scenes as these, can but behold in them the degradation of his own country, whose laws would make slaves of these same young men, should they appear in the streets of Charleston or New Orleans.

After all, our country is the most despotic in the wide world, and to expose and hold it up to the scorn and contempt of other nations, is the duty of every coloured man who would be true to himself and his race.

During my stay in Edinburgh, I accepted an invitation to breakfast with the great champion of Philosophical Phrenology. Few foreigners are more admired in America, than the author of "The Constitution of Man."[2] Although not far from 70 years of age, I found him apparently as active and as energetic as many men of half that age. He was much pleased with Mr. and Mrs. Craft, who formed a part of the breakfast party. It may be a pleasure to the friends of these two fugitive slaves, to know that they are now the inmates of a good school where they are now being educated. For this, they are mainly indebted to that untiring friend of the Slave, John B. Estlin, Esq., of Bristol, whose zeal and co-operation with the American Abolitionists, have gained for him an undying name with the friends of freedom in the New World.

LETTER XIII.

Edinburgh--The Royal Institute--Scott's Monument--John Knox's Pulpit--Temperance Meeting--Glasgow--Great Meeting in the City Hall.

EDINBURGH, *January 1, 1851*.

You will see by the date of this that I am spending my New-Year's-Day in the Scottish Capital, in company with our friend, William Craft. I came by invitation to attend a meeting of the Edinburgh Ladies' Emancipation Society.

The meeting was held on Monday evening last, at which William Craft gave, for the first time, since his arrival in this country, a history of his escape from Georgia, two years ago, together with his recent flight from Boston.

---

2   George Combe, Esq.

Craft's reception was one of deep enthusiasm, and his story was well told, and made a powerful impression on the audience. I would that the slaveholders, Hughes and Knight, could have been present and heard the thundering applause with which our friend was received on the following evening. Craft attended a meeting of the Edinburgh Total Abstinence Society, before which I lectured, and his appearance here was also hailed with much enthusiasm. Our friend bids fair to become a favourite with the Scotch.

Much regret was expressed that Ellen was not present. She was detained in Liverpool by indisposition. But Mrs. Craft has so far recovered, that we expect her here to-morrow.

The appearance of these two fugitives in Great Britain, at this time, and under the circumstances, will aid our cause, and create a renewed hatred to the abominable institution of American slavery. I have received letters from a number of the friends of the slave, in which they express a wish to aid the Crafts; and among the first of these, were our good friends, John B. Estlin, Esq., of Bristol, and Harriet Martineau.

But I must give you my impression of this fine city. Edinburgh is the most picturesque of all the towns which I have visited since my arrival in the father-land. Its situation has been compared to that of Athens, but it is said that the modern Athens is superior to the ancient. I was deeply impressed with the idea that I had seen the most beautiful of cities, after beholding those fashionable resorts, Paris and Versailles. I have seen nothing in the way of public grounds to compare with the gardens of Versailles, or the ***Champs Elysees*** at Paris; and as for statuary, the latter place is said to take the lead of the rest of the world.

The general appearance of Edinburgh prepossesses one in its favour. The town being built upon the brows of a large terrace, presents the most wonderful perspective. Its first appearance to a stranger, and the first impression, can scarcely be but favourable. In my first walk through the town, I was struck with the difference in the appearance of the people from the English. But the difference between the Scotch and the Americans, is very great. The cheerfulness depicted in the countenances of the people here, and their free and easy appearance, is very striking to a stranger. He who taught the sun to shine, the flowers to bloom, the birds to sing, and blesses us with rain, never intended that his creatures should look sad. There is a wide difference between the Americans and any other people which I have seen. The Scotch are healthy and robust, unlike the long-faced, sickly-looking Americans.

While on our journey from London to Paris, to attend the Peace Congress, I could not but observe the marked difference between the English and American delegates. The former looked as if their pockets had been filled with sandwiches, made of good bread and roast beef, while the latter appeared as if their pockets had been filled with Holloway's Pills, and Mrs. Kidder's Cordial.

I breakfasted this morning in a room in which the Poet Burns, as I was informed, had often sat. The conversation here turned upon Burns. The lady of the house pointed to a scrap of poetry which was in a frame hanging on the wall, written, as she said, by the Poet, on hearing the people rejoicing in a church over the intelligence of a victory. I copied it and will give it to you:--

> "Ye hypocrites! are these your pranks,
> To murder men and give God thanks?
> For shame! give o'er, proceed no further,
> God won't accept your thanks for murder."

The fact that I was in the room where Scotland's great national poet had been a visitor, caused me to feel that I was on classic, if not hallowed ground. On returning from our morning visit, we met a gentleman with a coloured lady on each arm. Craft remarked in a very dry manner, "If they were in Georgia, the slaveholders would make them walk in a more hurried gait than they do." I said to my friend, that if he meant the pro-slavery prejudice would not suffer them to walk peaceably through the streets, they need go no further than the pro-slavery cities of New York and Philadelphia. When walking through the streets, I amused myself, by watching Craft's countenance; and in doing so, imagined I saw the changes experienced by every fugitive slave in his first month's residence in this country. A sixteen months' residence has not yet familiarized me with the change.

* * * * *

LAUREL BANK, *Jan. 18, 1851*.

Dear Douglass,--I remained in Edinburgh a day or two after the date of my last letter, which gave me an opportunity of seeing some of the lions in the way of public buildings, &c., in company with our friend Wm. Craft. I paid a visit to the Royal Institute, and inspected the very fine collection of paintings, statues, and other productions of art. The collection in the Institute is not to be compared to the British Museum at London, or the Louvre at Paris, but is probably the best in Scotland. Paintings from the hands of many of the masters, such as Sir A. Vandyke, Tiziano, Vercellio and Van Dellen, were hanging on the wall, and even the names of Reubens, and Titian, were attached to some of the finer specimens. Many of these represent some of the nobles, and distinguished families of Rome, Athens, Greece, &c. A beautiful one representing a group of the Lomellini family of Genoa, seemed to attract the attention of most of the visitors.

In visiting this place, we passed close by the monument of Sir Walter Scott. This is the most exquisite thing of the kind that I have seen since coming to this country. It is said to be the finest monument in Europe. There sits the author of "Waverley," with a book and pencil in hand, taking notes. A beautiful dog is seated by his side. Whether this is meant to represent his favourite dog, Camp, at whose death the Poet shed so many tears, we were not informed; but I was of opinion that it might be the faithful Percy, whose monument stands in the grounds at Abbotsford. Scott was an admirer of the canine tribe. One may form a good idea of the appearance of this distinguished writer, when living, by viewing this remarkable statue. The statue is very beautiful, but not equal to the one of Lord Byron, which was executed to be placed by the side of Johnson, Milton, and Addison, in Poets' Corner, Westminster Abbey; but the Parliament not allowing it a place there, it now stands in one of the Colleges at Cambridge. While viewing the statue of Byron, I thought he, too, should have been represented with a dog by his side, for he, like Scott, was remarkably fond of dogs, so much so that he intended to have his favourite, Boatswain, interred by his side.

We paid a short visit to the monuments of Burns and Allan Ramsay, and the renowned old Edinburgh Castle. The Castle is now used as a barrack for Infantry. It is accessible only from the High Street, and must have been impregnable before the discovery of gunpowder. In the wars with the English, it was twice taken by stratagem; once in a very daring manner, by climbing up the most inaccessible part of the rock upon which it stands, and where a foe was least expected, and putting the guard to death; and another time, by a party of soldiers disguising themselves as merchants, and obtaining admission inside the Castle gates. They succeeded in preventing the gates from being closed, until reinforced by a party of men under Sir Wm. Douglas, who soon overpowered the occupants of the Castle.

We could not resist the temptation held out to see the Palace of Holyrood. It was in this place that the beautiful, but unfortunate Mary, Queen of Scots, resided for a number of years. On reaching the palace, we were met at the door by an elderly looking woman, with a red face, garnished with a pair of second-hand curls, the whole covered with a cap having the widest border that I had seen for years. She was very kind in showing us about the premises, especially as we were foreigners, no doubt expecting an extra fee for politeness. The most interesting of the many rooms in this ancient castle, is the one which was occupied by the Queen, and where her Italian favourite, Rizzio, was murdered.

But by far the most interesting object which we visited while in Edinburgh, was the house where the celebrated Reformer, John Knox, re-resided. It is a queer-looking old building, with a pulpit on the outside, and above the door are the nearly obliterated remains of the following inscription:--"Lufe. God. Above. Al. And. your. Nichbour. As you. Self." This was probably traced under the immediate direction of the great Reformer. Such an inscription put upon a house of worship at the present day, would be laughed at. I have given it to you, punctuation and all, just as it stands.

The general architecture of Edinburgh is very imposing, whether we regard the picturesque disorder of the buildings, in the Old Town, or the symmetrical proportions of the streets and squares in the New. But on viewing this city which has the reputation of being the finest in Europe, I was surprised to find that it had none of those sumptuous structures, which like St. Paul's, or Westminster Abbey, York Minster, and some other of the English provincial Cathedrals, astonish the beholder alike by their magnitude and their architectural splendour. But in no city which I have visited in the kingdom, is the general standard of excellence better maintained than in Edinburgh.

I am not sure, my dear friend, whether or not I mentioned in my last letter the attendance of Wm. Craft and myself at a splendid Soiree of the Edinburgh Temperance Society, and our being voted in life members, in the most enthusiastic manner, by the whole audience. I will here give you a part of the speech of the President, as reported in the ***Christian News***. This should cause the pro-slavery whites, and especially negro-hating Sons of Temperance, who refuse the coloured man a place in their midst, to feel ashamed of their unchristian conduct. Here it is, let them judge for themselves:--

"A great feature in our meeting to-night, is that we have beside us two individuals, who, according to the immaculate laws of immaculate Yankeedom, have been guilty of the tremendous crime of stealing themselves. (Applause.) Mr. Craft, who sits beside me, has stolen his good wife, and Mrs. Craft has stolen her worthy husband; and our respected friend, Mr. Brown, has cast a covetous eye on his own person. In the name of the Temperance reformers of Edinburgh--in the name of universal Scotland, I would welcome these two victims of the white man's pride, ambition, selfishness, and cupidity. I welcome them as our equals in every respect. (Great applause.) What a humiliating thought it will be, surely, for our American friends on the other side of the water, when they hear (and we shall endeavour to let them hear) that the very man whom they consider not worthy to sit in a third class carriage along with a white man, and that too in a district of country where the very aristocracy deal in cheap cheese--(great applause) traffic in tallow candles, and spend their nights and days among raw hides and train oil--(applause)--what a humbling thought it will be for them to know that these very men in the centre of educated Scotland, in the midst of educated Edinburgh, are thought fit to hold even the first rank upon our aristocratic platform. Let us, then, my friends, lift our voices this evening in one swelling chorus for the down-trodden slave. Let us publish abroad the fact to the world, that the sympathies of Scotland are with the bondsman everywhere. Let us unite our voices to cry, Down with the iniquitous Slave Bill!--Down with the aristocracy of the skin!--Perish forever the deepest-dyed, the hardest-hearted system of abomination under heaven!--Perish the sum of all villanies! Perish American slavery. (Great applause.)"

But I must leave the good and hospitable people of the Scottish Capital for the present. I have taken an elaborate stock of notes, and may speak of Edinburgh again.

I left William and Ellen Craft (the latter of whom has just come to Edinburgh), and took the Glasgow train, and after a ride of two hours through a beautiful country, with its winding hills on either side--its fertile fields, luxuriant woods, and stately mansions lying around us, arrived in the muddy, dirty, smoky, foggy city of Glasgow. As I had had a standing invitation from a distinguished gentleman with whom I became acquainted in London, to partake of his hospitality, should I ever visit Glasgow, and again received a note while in Edinburgh renewing the invitation, I proceeded to his residence at Partick, three miles from Glasgow. This is one of the loveliest spots which I have yet seen. Our mansion is on the side of Laurel Bank, a range of the Kilpatrick hills. We have a view of the surrounding country.

On Monday evening, Jan. 6, a public meeting was held in the City Hall, to extend a welcome to the American fugitive slaves. The hall, one of the largest in the kingdom, was filled at an early hour. At the appointed time, Alex. Hastie, Esq., M.P., entered the great room, followed by the fugitives and most of the leading abolitionists, amid rapturous applause. With a Member of Parliament in the chair, and almost any number of clergymen on the platform, the meeting had an influential appearance. From report, I had imbibed the opinion that the Scotch were not easily moved, but if I may judge from the enthusiasm which characterised the City Hall demonstration, I should place them but little behind the English. After an excellent speech from the Chairman, and spirited addresses from several clergymen, William Craft was introduced to the meeting, and gave an account of the escape of himself and wife from slavery, and their subsequent flight from Boston. Any description of mine would give but a poor idea of the intense feeling that pervaded the meeting. I think all who were there, left the hall after hearing that noble fugitive, with a greater abhorrence of American slavery than they previously entertained.

LETTER XIV.

Stirling--Dundee--Dr. Dick--Geo. Gilfillan--Dr. Dick at home.

PERTH, SCOTLAND, *Jan. 31, 1851.*

I am glad once more to breathe an atmosphere uncontaminated by the fumes and smoke of a city with its population of three hundred thousand inhabitants. In company with our friends Wm. and Ellen Craft, I left Glasgow on the afternoon of the 23d inst., for Dundee, a beautiful town situated on the banks of the river Tay. One like myself, who has spent the best part of an eventful life in cities, and who prefers, as I do, a country to a town life, feels a greater degree of freedom when surrounded by forest trees, or country dwellings, and looking upon a clear sky, than when walking through the thronged thoroughfares of a city, with its dense population, meeting every moment a new or strange face which one has never seen before, and never expects to see again. Although I had met with one of the warmest public receptions with which I have been greeted since my arrival in the country, and had had an opportunity of shaking hands with many noble friends of the slave, whose names I had often seen in print, yet I felt glad to see the tall chimneys and smoke of Glasgow receding in the distance, as our 'iron horse' was taking us with almost lightning speed from the commercial capital of Scotland.

The distance from Glasgow to Dundee is some seventy or eighty miles, and we passed through the finest country which I have seen in this portion of the Queen's dominions. We passed through the old town of Stirling, which lies about thirty miles distant from Glasgow, and is a place much frequented by those who travel for pleasure. It is built on the brow of a hill, and the Castle from which it most probably derived its name, may be seen from a distance. Had it not been for a "professional" engagement the same evening at Dundee, I would most assuredly have halted to take a look at the old building.

The Castle is situated or built on an isolated rock, which seems as if Nature had thrown it there for that purpose. It was once the retreat of the Scottish Kings, and famous for its historical associations. Here the "Lady of the Lake," with the magic ring, sought the monarch to intercede for her father; here James II. murdered the Earl of Douglas; here the beautiful but unfortunate Mary was made Queen; and here John Knox, the Reformer, preached the coronation sermon of James VI. The Castle Hill rises from the valley of the Forth, and makes an imposing and picturesque appearance. The windings of the noble river till lost in the distance, present pleasing contrasts, scarcely to be surpassed.

The speed of our train, after passing Stirling, brought before us, in quick succession, a number of fine valleys and farm houses. Every spot seemed to have been arrayed by Nature for the reception of the cottage of some happy family. During this ride, we passed many sites where the lawns were made, the terraces defined and levelled, the groves tastefully clumped, the ancient trees, though small when compared to our great forest oaks, were beautifully sprinkled here and there, and in everything the labour of art seemed to have been anticipated by Nature.

Cincinnatus could not have selected a prettier situation for a farm, than some which presented themselves, during this delightful journey. At last we arrived at the place of our destination, where our friends were in waiting for us.

As I have already forwarded to you a paper containing an account of the Dundee meeting, I shall leave you to judge from these reports the character of the demonstration. Yet I must mention a fact or two connected with our first evening's visit to this town. A few hours after our arrival in the place, we were called upon by a gentleman whose name is known wherever the English language is spoken--one whose name is on the tongue of every student and school-boy in this country and America, and what lives upon their lips will live and be loved for ever.

We were seated over a cup of strong tea, to revive our spirits for the evening, when our friend entered the room, accompanied by a gentleman, small in stature, and apparently seventy-five years of age, yet he appeared as active as one half that age. Feeling half drowsy from riding in the cold, and then the sudden change to a warm fire, I was rather inclined not to move on the entrance of the stranger. But the name of Thomas Dick, LL.D., roused me in a moment, from my lethargy; I could scarcely believe that I was in the presence of the "Christian Philosopher." Dr. Dick is one of the men to whom the age is indebted. I never find myself in the presence of one to whom the world owes so much as Dr. Dick, without feeling a thrilling emotion, as if I were in the land of spirits. Dr. Dick had come to our lodgings to see and congratulate Wm. and Ellen Craft upon their escape from the republican Christians of the United States; and as he pressed the hand of the "white slave," and bid her "welcome to British soil," I saw the silent tear stealing down the cheek of this man of genius. How I wished that the many slaveholders and pro-slavery professed Christians of America, who have read and pondered the philosophy of this man, could have been present. Thomas Dick is an abolitionist--one who is willing that the world should know that he hates the "peculiar institution." At the meeting that evening, Dr. Dick was among the most prominent. But this was not the only distinguished man who took part on that occasion.

Another great mind was on the platform, and entered his solemn protest in a manner long to be remembered by those present. This was the Rev. George Gilfillan, well known as the author of the "Portraits of Literary Men." Mr. Gilfillan is an energetic speaker, and would have been the lion of the evening, even if many others who are more distinguished as platform orators had been present. I think it was Napoleon who said that the enthusiasm of others abated his own. At any rate, the spirit with which each speaker entered upon his duty for the evening, abated my own enthusiasm for the time being. The last day of our stay in Dundee, I paid a visit, by invitation, to Dr. Dick, at his residence in the little village of Broughty Ferry. We found the great astronomer in his parlour waiting for us. From the parlour we went to the new study, and here I felt more at ease, for I went to see the Philosopher in his study, and not in his drawing-room. But even this room had too much the look of nicety to be an author's ***sanctum***; and I inquired and was soon informed by Mrs. Dick, that I should have a look at the "***old study***."

During a sojourn of eighteen months in Great Britain, I have had the good fortune to meet with several distinguished literary characters, and have always managed, while at their places of abode, to see the table and favourite chair. Wm. and Ellen Craft were seeing what they could see through a microscope, when Mrs. Dick returned to the room, and intimated that we could now see the old literary workshop. I followed, and was soon in a room about fifteen feet square, with but one window, which occupied one side of the room. The walls of the other three sides were lined with books. And many of these looked the very personification of age. I took my seat in the "***old arm chair***;" and here, thought I, is the place and the seat in which this distinguished man sat, while weaving the radiant wreath of renown which now in his old age surrounds him, and whose labours will be more appreciated by future ages than the present.

I took a farewell of the author of the "Solar System," but not until I had taken a look through the great telescope in the observatory. This instrument, through which I tried to see the heavens, was not the one invented by Galileo, but an improvement upon the original. On leaving this learned man, he shook hands with us, and bade us "God speed" in our mission; and I left the philosopher, feeling I had not passed an hour more agreeably, with a literary character, since the hour which I spent with Poet Montgomery a few months since. And, by-the-bye, there is a resemblance between the poet and the philosopher. In becoming acquainted with great men, I have become a convert to the opinion, that a big nose is an almost necessary appendage to the form of a man with a giant intellect. If those whom I have seen be a criterion, such is certainly the case. But I have spun out this too long, and must close.

LETTER XV.

Melrose Abbey--Abbotsford--Dryburgh Abbey--The Grave of Sir Walter Scott--Hawick--Gretna Green--Visit to the Lakes.

YORK, *March 26, 1851*.

I closed my last letter in the ancient town of Melrose, on the banks of the Tweed, and within a stone's throw of the celebrated ruins from which the town derives its name. The valley in which Melrose is situated, and the surrounding hills, together with the Monastery, have so often been made a theme for the Scottish bards, that this has become the most interesting part of Scotland. Of the many gifted writers who have taken up the pen, none have done more to bring the Eildon Hills and Melrose Abbey into note, than the author of "Waverley." But who can read his writings without a regret, that he should have so woven fact and fiction together, that it is almost impossible to discriminate between the one and the other.

We arrived at Melrose in the evening, and proceeded to the chapel where our meeting was to be held, and where our friends, the Crafts, were warmly greeted. On returning from the meeting, we passed close by the ruins of Melrose, and, very fortunately, it was a moonlight night. There is considerable difference of opinion among the inhabitants of the place as regards the best time to view the Abbey. The author of the "Lay of the Last Minstrel," says:--

> "If thou wouldst view fair Melrose aright,
> Go visit it by the pale moonlight:
> For the gay beams of lightsome day
> Gild but to flout the ruins gray."

In consequence of this admonition, I was informed that many persons remain in town to see the ruins by moonlight. Aware that the moon did not send its rays upon the old building every night in the year, I asked the keeper what he did on dark nights. He replied that he had a large lantern, which he put upon the end of a long pole, and with this he succeeded in lighting up the ruins. This good man laboured hard to convince me that his invention was nearly, if not quite as good, as Nature's own moon. But having no need of an application of his invention to the Abbey, I had no opportunity of judging of its effect. I thought, however, that he had made a moon to some purpose, when he informed me that some nights, with his pole and lantern, he earned his four or five shillings. Not being content with a view by "moonlight alone," I was up the next morning before the sun, and paid my respects to the Abbey. I was too early for the keeper, and he handed me the key through the window, and I entered the rooms alone. It is one labyrinth of gigantic arches and dilapidated halls, the ivy growing and clinging wherever it can fasten its roots, and the whole as fine a picture of decay as imagination could create. This was the favourite resort of Sir Walter Scott, and furnished him much matter for the "Lay of the Last Minstrel." He could not have selected a more fitting place for solitary thought than this ancient abode of monks and priests. In passing through the cloisters, I could not but remark the carvings of leaves and flowers, wrought in stone in the most exquisite manner, looking as fresh as if they were just from the hands of the artist. The lapse of centuries seems not to have made any impression upon them, or changed their appearance in the least. I sat down among the ruins of the Abbey. The ground about was piled up with magnificent fragments of stone, representing various texts of Scripture, and the quaint ideas of the priests and monks of that age. Scene after scene swept through my fancy as I looked upon the surrounding objects. I could almost imagine I saw the bearded monks going from hall to hall, and from cell to cell. In visiting these dark cells, the mind becomes oppressed by a sense of the utter helplessness of the victims who once passed over the thresholds and entered these religious prisons. There was no help or hope but in the will that ordered their fate. How painful it is to gaze upon these walls, and to think how many tears have been shed by their inmates, when this old Monastery was in its glory. I ascended to the top of the ruin by a circuitous stairway, whose stone steps were worn deep from use by many who, like myself, had visited them to gratify a curiosity. From the top of the Abbey, I had a splendid view of the surrounding hills and the beautiful valley through which flows the Gala Water and Tweed. This is unquestionably the most splendid specimen of Gothic architectural ruin in Scotland. But any description of mine conveys but a poor idea to the fancy. To be realized, it must be seen.

During the day, we paid a visit to Abbotsford, the splendid mansion of the late Sir Walter Scott, Bart. This beautiful seat is situated on the banks of the Tweed, just below its junction with the Gala Water. It is a dreary looking spot, and the house from the opposite side of the river has the appearance of a small, low castle. In a single day's ride through England, one may see half a dozen cottages larger than Abbotsford House. I was much disappointed in finding the premises undergoing repairs and alterations, and that all the trees between the house and the river had been cut down. This is to be regretted the more, because they were planted, nearly every one of them, by the same hand that waved its wand of enchantment over the world. The fountain had been removed from where it had been placed by the hands of the Poet to the centre of the yard; and even a small stone that had been placed over the favourite dog "Percy," had been taken up and thrown among some loose stones. One visits Abbotsford because of the genius of the man that once presided over it. Everything connected with the great Poet is of interest to his admirers, and anything altered or removed, tends to diminish that interest. We entered the house, and were conducted through the great Hall, which is hung all round with massive armour of all descriptions, and other memorials of ancient times. The floor is of white and black marble. In passing through the hall, we entered a narrow arched room, stretching quite across the building, having a window at each end. This little or rather narrow room is filled with all kinds of armour, which is arranged with great taste. We were next shown into the Dining-room, whose roof is of black oak, richly carved. In this room is a painting of the head of Queen Mary, in a charger, taken the day after the execution. Many other interesting portraits grace the walls of this room. But by far the finest apartment in the building is the Drawing-room, with a lofty ceiling, and furnished with antique ebony furniture. After passing through the Library, with its twenty thousand volumes, we found ourselves in the Study, and I sat down in the same chair where once sat the Poet; while before me was the table upon which was written the "Lady of the Lake," "Waverley," and other productions of this gifted writer. The clothes last worn by the Poet were shown to us. There was the broad skirted blue coat, with its large buttons, the plaid trousers, the heavy shoes, the black vest and white hat. These were all in a glass case, and all looked the poet and novelist. But the inside of the buildings had undergone alterations as well as the outside. In passing through the Library, we saw a granddaughter of the Poet. She was from London, and was only on a visit of a few days. She looked pale and dejected, and seemed as if she longed to leave this secluded spot and return to the metropolis. She looked for all the world like a hothouse plant. I don't think the Scotch could do better than to purchase Abbotsford, while it has some imprint of the great magician, and secure its preservation; for I am sure that, a hundred years hence, no place will be more frequently visited in Scotland than the home of the late Sir Walter Scott. After sauntering three hours about the premises, I left, but not without feeling that I had been well paid for my trouble in visiting Abbotsford.

In the afternoon of the same day, in company with the Crafts, I took a drive to Dryburgh Abbey. It is a ruin of little interest, except as being the burial place of Scott. The poet lies buried in St. Mary's Aisle. His grave is in the left transept of the cross, and close to where the high altar formerly stood. Sir Walter Scott chose his own grave, and he could not have selected a sunnier spot if he had roamed the wide world over. A shaded window breaks the sun as it falls upon his grave. The ivy is creeping and clinging wherever it can, as if it would shelter the poet's grave from the weather. The author lies between his wife and eldest son, and there is only room enough for one grave more, and the son's wife has the choice of being buried here.

The four o'clock train took us to Hawick; and after a pleasant visit in this place, and the people registering their names against American Slavery, and the Fugitive Bill in particular, we set out for Carlisle, passing through the antique town of Langholm. After leaving the latter place, we had to travel by coach. But no matter how one travels here, he travels at a more rapid rate than in America. The distance from Langholm to Carlisle, twenty miles, occupied only two and a-half hours in the journey. It was a cold day and I had to ride on the outside, as the inside had been taken up. We changed horses, and took in and put out passengers with a rapidity which seems almost incredible. The road was as smooth as a mirror.

We bid farewell to Scotland, as we reached the little town of Gretna Green. This town being on the line between England and Scotland, is noted as the place where a little cross-eyed, red-faced blacksmith, by the name of Priestly, first set up his own altar to Hymen, and married all who came to him, without regard to rank or station, and at prices to suit all. It was worth a ride through this part of the country, if for no other purpose than to see the town where more clandestine marriages have taken place than in any other part in the world. A ride of eight or nine miles brought us in sight of the Eden, winding its way slowly through a beautiful valley, with farms on either side, covered with sheep and cattle. Four very tall chimneys, sending forth dense columns of black smoke, announced to us that we were near Carlisle. I was really glad of this, for Ulysses was never more tired of the shores of Ilion than I of the top of that coach.

We remained over night at Carlisle, partaking of the hospitality of the prince of bakers, and left the next day for the Lakes, where we had a standing invitation to pay a visit to a distinguished literary lady. A cold ride of about fifty miles brought us to the foot of Lake Windermere, a beautiful sheet of water, surrounded by mountains that seemed to vie with each other which should approach nearest the sky. The margin of the lake is carved out and built up into terrace above terrace, until the slopes and windings are lost in the snow-capped peaks of the mountains. It is not surprising that such men as Southey, Coleridge, Wordsworth, and others, resorted to this region for inspiration. After a coach ride of five miles (passing on our journey the "Dove's Nest," home of the late Mrs. Hemans), we were put down at the door of the Salutation Hotel, Ambleside, and a few minutes after found ourselves under the roof of the authoress of "Society in America." I know not how it is with others, but for my own part, I always form an opinion of the appearance of an author whose writings I am at all familiar with, or a statesman whose speeches I have read. I had pictured in my own mind a tall, stately-looking lady of about sixty years, as the authoress of "Travels in the East," and for once I was right, with the single exception that I had added on too many years by twelve. The evening was spent in talking about the United States; and William Craft had to go through the narrative of his escape from slavery. When I retired for the night, I found it almost impossible to sleep. The idea that I was under the roof of the authoress of "The Hour and the Man," and that I was on the banks of the sweetest lake in Great Britain, within half a mile of the residence of the late poet Wordsworth, drove sleep from my pillow. But I must leave an account of my visit to the Lakes for a future letter.

When I look around and see the happiness here, even among the poorer classes, and that too in a country where the soil is not at all to be compared with our own, I mourn for our down-trodden countrymen, who are plundered, oppressed, and made chattels of, to enable an ostentatious aristocracy to vie with each other in splendid extravagance.

LETTER XVI.

Miss Martineau--"The Knoll"--"Ridal Mount"--"The Dove's Nest"--Grave of William Wordsworth, Esq.--The English Peasant.

May 30, 1851.

A series of public meetings, one pressing close upon the heel of another, must be an apology for my six or eight weeks' silence. But I hope that no temporary suspense on my part will be construed into a want of interest in our cause, or a wish to desist from giving occasionally a scrap (such as it is) to the ***North Star***.

My last letter left me under the hospitable roof of Harriet Martineau. I had long had an invitation to visit this distinguished friend of our race, and as the invitation was renewed during my tour through the North, I did not feel disposed to decline it, and thereby lose so favourable an opportunity of meeting with one who had written so much in behalf of the oppressed of our land. About a mile from the head of Lake Windermere, and immediately under Wonsfell, and encircled by mountains on all sides, except the south-west, lies the picturesque little town of Ambleside, and the brightest spot in the place is "The Knoll," the residence of Miss Martineau.

We reached "The Knoll" a little after nightfall, and a cordial shake of the hand by Miss M., who was waiting for us, soon assured us that we had met with a warm friend.

It is not my intention to lay open the scenes of domestic life at "The Knoll," nor to describe the social parties of which my friends and I were partakers during our sojourn within the hospitable walls of this distinguished writer; but the name of Miss M. is so intimately connected with the Anti-slavery movement, by her early writings, and those have been so much admired by the friends of the slave in the United States, that I deem it not at all out of place for me to give the readers of the ***North Star*** some idea of the authoress of "Political Economy," "Travels in the East," "The Hour and the Man," &c.

The dwelling is a cottage of moderate size, built after Miss M.'s own plan, upon a rise of land from which it derives the name of "The Knoll." The Library is the largest room in the building, and upon the walls of it were hung some beautiful engravings and a continental map. On a long table which occupied the centre of the room, were the busts of Shakspere, Newton, Milton, and a few other literary characters of the past. One side of the room was taken up with a large case, filled with a choice collection of books, and everything indicated that it was the home of genius and of taste.

The room usually occupied by Miss M., and where we found her on the evening of our arrival, is rather small and lighted by two large windows. The walls of this room were also decorated with prints and pictures, and on the mantle-shelf were some models in **terra cottia** of Italian groups. On a circular table lay casts, medallions, and some very choice water-colour drawings. Under the south window stood a small table covered with newly opened letters, a portfolio and several new books, with here and there a page turned down, and one with a paper knife between its leaves as if it had only been half read. I took up the last mentioned, and it proved to be the "Life and Poetry of Hartly Coleridge," son of S.T. Coleridge. It was just from the press, and had, a day or two before, been forwarded to her by the publisher. Miss M. is very deaf and always carries in her left hand a trumpet; and I was not a little surprised on learning from her that she had never enjoyed the sense of smell, and only on one occasion the sense of taste, and that for a single moment. Miss M. is loved with a sort of idolatry by the people of Ambleside, and especially the poor, to whom she gives a course of lectures every winter gratuitously. She finished her last course the day before our arrival. She was much pleased with Ellen Craft, and appeared delighted with the story of herself and husband's escape from slavery, as related by the latter--during the recital of which I several times saw the silent tear stealing down her cheek, and which she tried in vain to hide from us.

When Craft had finished, she exclaimed, "I would that every woman in the British Empire, could hear that tale as I have, so that they might know how their own sex was treated in that boasted land of liberty." It seems strange to the people of this county, that one so white and so lady-like as Mrs. Craft, should have been a slave and forced to leave the land of her nativity and seek an asylum in a foreign country. The morning after our arrival, I took a stroll by a circuitous pathway to the top of Loughrigg Fell. At the foot of the mount I met a peasant, who very kindly offered to lend me his donkey, upon which to ascend the mountain. Never having been upon the back of one of these long eared animals, I felt some hesitation about trusting myself upon so diminutive looking a creature. But being assured that if I would only resign myself to his care and let him have his own way, I would be perfectly safe, I mounted, and off we set. We had, however, scarcely gone fifty rods, when, in passing over a narrow part of the path and overlooking a deep chasm, one of the hind feet of the donkey slipped, and with an involuntary shudder, I shut my eyes to meet my expected doom; but fortunately the little fellow gained his foothold, and in all probability saved us both from a premature death. After we had passed over this dangerous place, I dismounted, and as soon as my feet had once more gained ***terra firma***, I resolved that I would never again yield my own judgment to that of any one, not even to a donkey.

It seems as if Nature has amused herself in throwing these mountains together. From the top of the Loughrigg Fell, the eye loses its power in gazing upon the objects below. On our left, lay Rydal Mount, the beautiful seat of the late poet Wordsworth. While to the right, and away in the dim distance, almost hidden by the native trees, was the cottage where once resided Mrs. Hemans. And below us lay Windermere, looking more like a river than a lake, and which, if placed by the side of our own Ontario, Erie or Huron, would be lost in the fog. But here it looks beautiful in the extreme, surrounded as it is by a range of mountains that have no parallel in the United States for beauty. Amid a sun of uncommon splendour, dazzling the eye with the reflection upon the water below, we descended into the valley, and I was soon again seated by the fireside of our hospitable hostess. In the afternoon of the same day, we took a drive to the "Dove's Nest," the home of the late Mrs. Hemans.

We did not see the inside of the house, on account of its being occupied by a very eccentric man, who will not permit a woman to enter the house, and it is said that he has been known to run when a female had unconsciously intruded herself upon his premises. And as our company was in part composed of ladies, we had to share their fate, and therefore were prevented from seeing the interior of the Dove's Nest. The exhibitor of such a man would be almost sure of a prize at the great Exhibition.

At the head of Grassmere Lake, and surrounded by a few cottages, stands an old gray, antique-looking Parish Church, venerable with the lapse of centuries, and the walls partly covered with ivy, and in the rear of which is the parish burial-ground. After leaving the Dove's Nest, and having a pleasant ride over the hills and between the mountains, and just as the sun was disappearing behind them, we arrived at the gate of Grassmere Church; and alighting and following Miss M., we soon found ourselves standing over a grave, marked by a single stone, and that, too, very plain, with a name deeply cut. This announced to us that we were standing over the grave of William Wordsworth. He chose his own grave, and often visited the spot before his death. He lies in the most sequestered spot in the whole grounds, and the simplicity and beauty of the place was enough to make one in love with it, to be laid so far from the bustle of the world, and in so sweet a place. The more one becomes acquainted with the literature of the old world, the more he must love her poets. Among the teachers of men, none are more worthy of study than the poets; and, as teachers, they should receive far more credit than is yielded to them. No one can look back upon the lives of Dante, Shakspere, Milton, Goethe, Cowper, and many others that we might name, without being reminded of the sacrifices which they made for mankind, and which were not appreciated until long after their deaths. We need look no farther than our own country to find men and women wielding the pen practically and powerfully for the right. It is acknowledged on all hands in this country, that England has the greatest dead poets, and America the greatest living ones. The poet and the true Christian have alike a hidden life. Worship is the vital element of each. Poetry has in it that kind of utility which good men find in their Bible, rather than such convenience as bad men often profess to draw from it. It ennobles the sentiments, enlarges the affections, kindles the imagination, and gives to us the enjoyment of a life in the past, and in the future, as well as in the present. Under its light and warmth, we wake from our torpidity and coldness, to a sense of our capabilities. This impulse once given, a great object is gained. Schiller has truly said, "Poetry can be to a man, what love is to a hero. It can neither counsel him nor smite him, nor perform any labour for him, but it can bring him up to be a hero, can summon him to deeds, and arm him with strength for all he ought to be." I have often read with pleasure the sweet poetry of our own Whitfield of Buffalo, which has appeared from time to time in the columns of the ***North Star***. I have always felt ashamed of the fact that he should be compelled to wield the razor instead of the pen for a living. Meaner poets than James M. Whitfield, are now living by their compositions; and were he a white man he would occupy a different position.

After remaining a short time, and reading the epitaphs of the departed, we again returned to "The Knoll." Nothing can be more imposing than the beauty of English park scenery, and especially in the vicinity of the lakes. Magnificent lawns that extend like sheets of vivid green, with here and there a sprinkling of fine trees, heaping up rich piles of foliage, and then the forests with the hare, the deer, and the rabbit, bounding away to the covert, or the pheasant suddenly bursting upon the wing--the artificial stream, the brook taught to wind in natural meanderings, or expand into the glassy lake, with the yellow leaf sleeping upon its bright waters, and occasionally a rustic temple or sylvan statue grown green and dark with age, give an air of sanctity and picturesque beauty to English scenery that is unknown in the United States. The very labourer with his thatched cottage and narrow slip of ground-plot before the door, the little flower-bed, the woodbine trimmed against the wall, and hanging its blossoms about the windows, and the peasant seen trudging home at nightfall with the avails of the toil of the day upon his back--all this tells us of the happiness both of rich and poor in this country. And yet there are those who would have the world believe that the labourer of England is in a far worse condition than the slaves of America. Such persons know nothing of the real condition of the working classes of this country. At any rate, the poor here, as well as the rich, are upon a level, as far as the laws of the country are concerned. The more one becomes acquainted with the English people, the more one has to admire them. They are so different from the people of our own country. Hospitality, frankness, and good humour, are always to be found in an Englishman. After a ramble of three days about the lakes, we mounted the coach, bidding Miss Martineau farewell, and quitted the lake district.

LETTER XVII.

A Day in the Crystal Palace.

LONDON, *June 27th, 1851*.

Presuming that you will expect from me some account of the great World's Fair, I take my pen to give you my own impressions, although I am afraid that anything which I may say about this "Lion of the day," will fall far short of a description. On Monday last, I quitted my lodgings at an early hour, and started for the Crystal Palace. This day was fine, such as we seldom experience in London, with a clear sky, and invigorating air, whose vitality was as rousing to the spirits as a blast from the "horn of Astolpho." Although it was not yet 10 o'clock when I entered Piccadilly, every omnibus was full, inside and out, and the street was lined with one living stream, as far as the eye could reach, all wending their way to the "Glass-House." No metropolis in the world presents such facilities as London for the reception of the Great Exhibition, now collected within its walls. Throughout its myriads of veins, the stream of industry and toil pulses with sleepless energy. Every one seems to feel that this great Capital of the world, is the fittest place wherein they might offer homage to the dignity of toil. I had already begun to feel fatigued by my pedestrian excursion as I passed "Apsley House," the residence of the Duke of Wellington, and emerged into Hyde Park.

I had hoped that on getting into the Park, I would be out of the crowd that seemed to press so heavily in the street. But in this I was mistaken. I here found myself surrounded by and moving with an overwhelming mass, such as I had never before witnessed. And, away in the distance, I beheld a dense crowd, and above every other object, was seen the lofty summit of the Crystal Palace. The drive in the Park was lined with princely-looking vehicles of every description. The drivers in their bright red and gold uniforms, the pages and footmen in their blue trousers and white silk stockings, and the horses dressed up in their neat, silver-mounted harness, made the scene altogether one of great splendour. I was soon at the door, paid my shilling, and entered the building at the south end of the Transept. For the first ten or twenty minutes I was so lost in astonishment, and absorbed in pleasing wonder, that I could do nothing but gaze up and down the vista of the noble building. The Crystal Palace resembles in some respects, the interior of the cathedrals of this country. One long avenue from east to west is intersected by a Transept, which divides the building into two nearly equal parts. This is the greatest building the world ever saw, before which the Pyramids of Egypt, and the Colossus of Rhodes must hide their diminished heads. The palace was not full at any time during the day, there being only 64,000 persons present. Those who love to study the human countenance in all its infinite varieties, can find ample scope for the indulgence of their taste, by a visit to the World's Fair. All countries are there represented--Europeans, Asiatics, Americans and Africans, with their numerous subdivisions. Even the exclusive Chinese, with his hair braided, and hanging down his back, has left the land of his nativity, and is seen making long strides through the Crystal Palace, in his wooden-bottomed shoes. Of all places of curious costumes and different fashions, none has ever yet presented such a variety as this Exhibition. No dress is too absurd to be worn in this place.

There is a great deal of freedom in the Exhibition. The servant who walks behind his mistress through the Park feels that he can crowd against her in the Exhibition. The Queen and the day labourer, the Prince and the merchant, the peer and the pauper, the Celt and the Saxon, the Greek and the Frank, the Hebrew and the Russ, all meet here upon terms of perfect equality. This amalgamation of rank, this kindly blending of interests, and forgetfulness of the cold formalities of ranks and grades, cannot but be attended with the very best results. I was pleased to see such a goodly sprinkling of my own countrymen in the Exhibition--I mean coloured men and women--well-dressed, and moving about with their fairer brethren. This, some of our pro-slavery Americans did not seem to relish very well. There was no help for it. As I walked through the American part of the Crystal Palace, some of our Virginian neighbours eyed me closely and with jealous looks, especially as an English lady was leaning on my arm. But their sneering looks did not disturb me in the least. I remained the longer in their department, and criticised the bad appearance of their goods the more. Indeed, the Americans, as far as appearance goes, are behind every other country in the Exhibition. The "Greek Slave" is the only production of Art which the United States has sent. And it would have been more to their credit had they kept that at home. In so vast a place as the Great Exhibition one scarcely knows what to visit first, or what to look upon last. After wandering about through the building for five hours, I sat down in one of the galleries and looked at the fine marble statue of Virginius, with the knife in his hand and about to take the life of his beloved and beautiful daughter, to save her from the hands of Appius Claudius. The admirer of genius will linger for hours among the great variety of statues in the long avenue. Large statues of Lords Eldon and Stowell, carved out of solid marble, each weighing above twenty tons, are among the most gigantic in the building.

I was sitting with my 400 paged guide-book before me, and looking down upon the moving mass, when my attention was called to a small group of gentlemen standing near the statue of Shakspere, one of whom wore a white coat and hat, and had flaxen hair, and trousers rather short in the legs. The lady by my side, and who had called my attention to the group, asked if I could tell what country this odd-looking gentleman was from? Not wishing to run the risk of a mistake, I was about declining to venture an opinion, when the reflection of the sun against a mirror, on the opposite side, threw a brilliant light upon the group, and especially on the face of the gentleman in the white coat, and I immediately recognized under the brim of the white hat, the features of Horace Greeley, Esq., of the New York "Tribune." His general appearance was as much out of the English style as that of the Turk whom I had seen but a moment before--in his bag-like trousers, shuffling along in his slippers. But oddness in dress, is one of the characteristics of the Great Exhibition.

Among the many things in the Crystal Palace, there are some which receive greater attention than others, around which may always be seen large groups of the visitors. The first of these is the Koh-i-noor, the "Mountain of Light." This is the largest and most valuable diamond in the world, said to be worth L2,000,000 sterling. It is indeed a great source of attraction to those who go to the Exhibition for the first time, but it is doubtful whether it obtains such admiration afterwards. We saw more than one spectator turn away with the idea that after all it was only a piece of glass. After some jamming, I got a look at the precious jewel, and although in a brass-grated cage, strong enough to hold a lion, I found it to be no larger than the third of a hen's egg. Two policemen remain by its side day and night.

The finest thing in the Exhibition, is the "Veiled Vestal," a statue of a woman carved in marble, with a veil over her face, and so neatly done, that it looks as if it had been thrown over after it was finished. The Exhibition presents many things which appeal to the eye and touch the heart, and altogether, it is so decorated and furnished, as to excite the dullest mind, and satisfy the most fastidious.

England has contributed the most useful and substantial articles; France, the most beautiful; while Russia, Turkey, and the West Indies, seem to vie with each other in richness. China and Persia are not behind. Austria has also contributed a rich and beautiful stock. Sweden,

Norway, Denmark, and the smaller states of Europe, have all tried to outdo themselves in sending goods to the World's Fair. In Machinery, England has no competitor. In Art, France is almost alone in the Exhibition, setting aside England.

In natural productions and provisions, America stands alone in her glory. There lies her pile of canvassed hams; whether they were wood or real, we could not tell. There are her barrels of salt, beef, and pork, her beautiful white lard, her Indian-corn and corn-meal, her rice and tobacco, her beef tongues, dried peas, and a few bags of cotton. The contributors from the United States seemed to have forgotten that this was an exhibition of Art, or they most certainly would not have sent provisions. But the United States takes the lead in the contributions, as no other country has sent in provisions. The finest thing contributed by our countrymen, is a large piece of silk with an eagle painted upon it, surrounded by stars and stripes.

After remaining more than five hours in the great temple, I turned my back upon the richly laden stalls and left the Crystal Palace. On my return home I was more fortunate than in the morning, inasmuch as I found a seat for my friend and myself in an omnibus. And even my ride in the close omnibus was not without interest. For I had scarcely taken my seat, when my friend, who was seated opposite me, with looks and gesture informed me that we were in the presence of some distinguished person. I eyed the countenances of the different persons, but in vain, to see if I could find any one who by his appearance showed signs of superiority over his fellow-passengers. I had given up the hope of selecting the person of note when another look from my friend directed my attention to a gentlemen seated in the corner of the omnibus. He was a tall man with strongly marked features, hair dark and coarse. There was a slight stoop of the shoulder--that bend which is almost always a characteristic of studious men. But he wore upon his countenance a forbidding and disdainful frown, that seemed to tell one that he thought himself better than those about him. His dress did not indicate a man of high rank; and had we been in America, I would have taken him for an Ohio farmer.

While I was scanning the features and general appearance of the gentleman, the Omnibus stopped and put down three or four of the passengers, which gave me an opportunity of getting a seat by the side of my friend, who, in a low whisper, informed me that the gentleman whom I had been eyeing so closely, was no less a person than Thomas Carlyle. I had read his "Hero-worship," and "Past and Present," and had formed a high opinion of his literary abilities. But his recent attack upon the emancipated people of the West Indies, and his laborious article in favour of the re-establishment of the lash and slavery, had created in my mind a dislike for the man, and I almost regretted that we were in the same Omnibus. In some things, Mr. Carlyle is right: but in many, he is entirely wrong. As a writer, Mr. Carlyle is often monotonous and extravagant. He does not exhibit a new view of nature, or raise insignificant objects into importance, but generally takes commonplace thoughts and events, and tries to express them in stronger and statelier language than others. He holds no communion with his kind, but stands alone without mate or fellow. He is like a solitary peak, all access to which is cut off. He exists not by sympathy but by antipathy. Mr. Carlyle seems chiefly to try how he shall display his own powers, and astonish mankind, by starting new trains of speculation or by expressing old ones so as not to be understood. He cares little what he says, so as he can say it differently from others. To read his works, is one thing; to understand them, is another. If any one thinks that I exaggerate, let him sit for an hour over "Sartor Resartus," and if he does not rise from its pages, place his three or four dictionaries on the shelf, and say I am right, I promise never again to say a word against Thomas Carlyle. He writes one page in favour of Reform, and ten against it. He would hang all prisoners to get rid of them, yet the inmates of the prisons and "work-houses are better off than the poor." His heart is with the poor;

yet the blacks of the West Indies should be taught, that if they will not raise sugar and cotton by their own free will, "Quashy should have the whip applied to him." He frowns upon the Reformatory speakers upon the boards of Exeter Hall, yet he is the prince of reformers. He hates heroes and assassins, yet Cromwell was an angel, and Charlotte Corday a saint. He scorns everything, and seems to be tired of what he is by nature, and tries to be what he is not. But you will ask, what has Thomas Carlyle to do with a visit to the Crystal Palace? My only reply is, "Nothing," and if my remarks upon him have taken up the space that should have been devoted to the Exhibition, and what I have written not prove too burdensome to read, my next will be "a week in the Crystal Palace."

LETTER XVIII.

The London Peace Congress--Meeting of Fugitive Slaves--Temperance Demonstration--The Great Exhibition: last visit.

LONDON, *August 20*.

The past six weeks have been of a stirring nature in this great metropolis. It commenced with the Peace Congress, the proceedings of which have long since reached you. And although that event has passed off, it may not be out of place here to venture a remark or two upon its deliberations.

A meeting upon the subject of Peace, with the support of the monied and influential men who rally around the Peace standard, could scarcely have been held in Exeter Hall without creating some sensation. From all parts of the world flocked delegates to this practical protest against war. And among those who took part in the proceedings, were many men whose names alone would, even on ordinary occasions, have filled the great hall. The speakers were chosen from among the representatives of the various countries, without regard to dialect or complexion; and the only fault which seemed to be found with the Committee's arrangement was, that in their desire to get foreigners and Londoners, they forgot the country delegates, so that none of the large provincial towns were at all represented in the Congress, so far as speaking was concerned. Manchester, Leeds, Newcastle, and all the important towns in Scotland and Ireland, were silenced in the great meeting. I need not say that this was an oversight of the Committee, and one, too, that has done some injury. Such men as the able Chairman of the late Anti-Corn Law League, cannot be forgotten in such a meeting, without giving offence to those who sent him, especially when the Committee brought forward, day after day, the same speakers, chosen from amongst the metropolitan delegation. However, the meeting was a glorious one, and will long be remembered with delight as a step onward in the cause of Peace. Burritt's Brotherhood Bazaar followed close upon the heels of the Peace Congress; and this had scarcely closed, when that ever-memorable meeting of the American Fugitive Slaves took place in the Hall of Commerce.

The Temperance people made the next reformatory move. This meeting took place in Exeter Hall, and was made up of delegates from the various towns in the kingdom. They had come from the North, East, West, and South. There was the quick-spoken son of the Emerald Isle, with his pledge suspended from his neck; there, too, the Scot, speaking his broad dialect; also the representatives from the provincial towns of England and Wales, who seemed to speak anything but good English.

The day after the meeting had closed in Exeter Hall, the country societies, together with those of the metropolis, assembled in Hyde Park, and then walked to the Crystal Palace. Their number while going to the Exhibition, was variously estimated at from 15,000 to 20,000, and was said to have been the largest gathering of Teetotalers ever assembled in London. They consisted chiefly of the working classes, their wives and children--clean, well-dressed and apparently happy: their looks indicating in every way those orderly habits which, beyond question, distinguish the devotees of that cause above the common labourers of this country. On arriving at the Exhibition, they soon distributed themselves among the departments, to revel in its various wonders, eating their own lunch, and drinking from the Crystal Fountain.

And now I am at the world's wonder, I will remain here until I finish this sheet. I have spent fifteen days in the Exhibition, and have conversed with those who have spent double that number amongst its beauties, and the general opinion appears to be, that six months would not be too long to remain within its walls to enable one to examine its laden stalls. Many persons make the Crystal Palace their home, with the exception of night. I have seen them come in the morning, visit the dressing-room, then go to the refreshment room, and sit down to breakfast as if they had been at their hotel. Dinner and tea would be taken in turn.

The Crystal Fountain is the great place of meeting in the Exhibition. There you may see husbands looking for lost wives, wives for stolen husbands, mothers for their lost children, and towns-people for their country friends; and unless you have an appointment at a certain place at an hour, you might as well prowl through the streets of London to find a friend, as in the Great Exhibition. There is great beauty in the "Glass House." Here, in the transept, with the glorious sunlight coming through that wonderful glass roof, may the taste be cultivated and improved, the mind edified, and the feelings chastened. Here, surrounded by noble creations in marble and bronze, and in the midst of an admiring throng, one may gaze at statuary which might fitly decorate the house of the proudest prince in Christendom.

He who takes his station in the gallery, at either end, and looks upon that wondrous nave, or who surveys the matchless panorama around him from the intersection of the nave and transept, may be said, without presumption or exaggeration, to see all the kingdoms of this world and the glory of them. He sees not only a greater collection of fine articles, but also a greater as well as more various assemblage of the human race, than ever before was gathered under one roof.

One of the beauties of this great international gathering is, that it is not confined to rank or grade. The million toilers from mine, and factory, and workshop, and loom, and office, and field, share with their more wealthy neighbours the feast of reason and imagination spread out in the Crystal Palace.

It is strange indeed to see so many nations assembled and represented on one spot of British ground. In short, it is one great theatre, with thousands of performers, each playing his own part. England is there, with her mighty engines toiling and whirring, indefatigable in her enterprises to shorten labour. India spreads her glitter and paint. France, refined and fastidious, is there every day, giving the last touch to her picturesque group; and the other countries, each in their turn, doing what they can to show off. The distant hum of thousands of good humoured people, with occasionally a national anthem from some gigantic organ, together with the noise of the machinery, seems to send life into every part of the Crystal Palace.

When you get tired of walking, you can sit down and write your impressions, and there is the "post" to receive your letter, or if it be Friday or Saturday, you may, if you choose, rest yourself by hearing a lecture from Professor Anstead; and then before leaving take your last look, and see something that you have not before seen. Every thing which is old in cities, new in colonial life, splendid in courts, useful in industry, beautiful in nature, or ingenious in invention, is there represented. In one place we have the Bible translated into one hundred and fifty languages; in another, we have saints and archbishops painted on glass; in another, old palaces and the altars of a John Knox, a Baxter, or some other divines of olden time. In the old Temple of Delphi, we read that every state of the civilized world had its separate treasury, where Herodotus, born two thousand years before his time, saw and observed all kinds of prodigies in gold and silver, brass and iron, and even in linen. The nations all met there on one common ground, and the peace of the earth was not a little promoted by their common interest in the sanctity and splendour of that shrine. As long as the Exhibition lasts, and its memory endures, we hope and trust that it may shed the same influence. With this hasty scrap, I take leave of the Great Exhibition.

LETTER XIX.

Oxford--Martyrs' Monument--Cost of the Burning of the Martyrs--The Colleges--Dr. Pusey--Energy, the Secret of Success.

OXFORD, *September 10th, 1851*.

I have just finished a short visit to the far famed city of Oxford, which has not unaptly been styled the City of Palaces. Aside from this being one of the principal seats of learning in the world, it is distinguished alike for its religious and political changes in times past. At one time it was the seat of Popery; at another, the uncompromising enemy of Rome. Here the tyrant, Richard the Third, held his court, and when James the First, and his son Charles the First, found their capital too hot to hold them, they removed to their loyal city of Oxford. The writings of the great Republicans were here committed to the flames. At one time Popery sent Protestants to the stake and faggot; at another, a Papist King found no favour with the people. A noble monument now stands where Cranmer, Ridley, and Latimer, proclaimed their sentiments and faith, and sealed them with their blood. And now we read upon the Town Treasurer's book--for three loads of wood, one load of faggots, one post, two chains and staples, to burn Ridley and Latimer, L1 5s. 1d. Such is the information one gets by looking over the records of books written three centuries ago.

It was a beautiful day on which I arrived at Oxford, and instead of remaining in my hotel, I sallied forth to take a survey of the beauties of the city. I strolled into Christ Church Meadows, and there spent the evening in viewing the numerous halls of learning which surround that splendid promenade. And fine old buildings they are: centuries have rolled over many of them, hallowing the old walls, and making them grey with age. They have been for ages the chosen homes of piety and philosophy. Heroes and scholars have gone forth from their studies here, into the great field of the world, to seek their fortunes, and to conquer and be conquered. As I surveyed the exterior of the different Colleges, I could here and there see the reflection of the light from the window of some student, who was busy at his studies, or throwing away his time over some trashy novel, too many of which find their way into the trunks or carpet bags of the young men on setting out for College. As I looked upon the walls of these buildings, I thought as the rough stone is taken from the quarry to the finisher, there to be made into an ornament, so was the young mind brought here to be cultivated and developed. Many a poor unobtrusive young man, with the appearance of little or no ability, is here moulded into a hero, a scholar, a tyrant, or a friend of humanity. I never look upon these monuments of education, without a feeling of regret, that so few of our own race can find a place within their walls. And this being the fact, I see more and more the need of our people being encouraged to turn their attention more seriously to self-education, and thus to take a respectable position before the world, by virtue of their own cultivated minds and moral standing.

Education, though obtained by a little at a time, and that, too, over the midnight lamp, will place its owner in a position to be respected by all, even though he be black. I know that the obstacles which the laws of the land, and of society, place between the coloured man and education in the United States, are very great, yet if ***one*** can break through these barriers, more can; and if our people would only place the right appreciation upon education, they would find these obstacles are easier to be overcome than at first sight appears. A young man once asked Carlyle, what was the secret of success. His reply was, "Energy; whatever you undertake, do it with all your might." Had it not been for the possession of energy, I might now have been working as a servant for some brainless fellow who might be able to command my labour with his money, or I might have been yet toiling in chains and slavery. But thanks to energy, not only for my being to-day in a land of freedom, but also for my dear girls being in one of the best seminaries in France, instead of being in an American school, where the finger of scorn would be pointed at them by those whose superiority rests entirely upon their having a whiter skin. But I am straying too far from the purpose of this letter.

Oxford is indeed one of the finest located places in the kingdom, and every inch of ground about it seems hallowed by interesting associations. The University, founded by the good King Alfred, still throws its shadow upon the side-walk; and the lapse of ten centuries seems to have made but little impression upon it. Other seats of learning may be entitled to our admiration, but Oxford claims our veneration. Although the lateness of the night compelled me, yet I felt an unwillingness to tear myself from the scene of such surpassing interest. Few places in any country as noted as Oxford is, but what has some distinguished person residing within its precincts. And knowing that the City of Palaces was not an exception to this rule, I resolved to see some of its lions. Here, of course, is the head quarters of the Bishop of Oxford, a son of the late William Wilberforce, Africa's noble champion. I should have been glad to have seen this distinguished pillar of the Church, but I soon learned that the Bishop's residence was out of town, and that he seldom visited the city except on business. I then determined to see one who, although a lesser dignitary in the church, is nevertheless, scarcely less known than the Bishop of Oxford. This was the Rev. Dr. Pusey, a divine, whose name is known wherever the religion of Jesus is known and taught, and the acknowledged head of the Puseyites. On the second morning of my visit, I proceeded to Christ Church Chapel, where the rev. gentleman officiates. Fortunately I had an opportunity of seeing the Dr., and following close in his footsteps to the church. His personal appearance is anything but that of one who is the leader of a growing and powerful party in the church. He is rather under the middle size, and is round shouldered, or rather stoops. His profile is more striking than his front face, the nose being very large and prominent. As a matter of course, I expected to see a large nose, for all great men have them. He has a thoughtful, and somewhat sullen brow, a firm and somewhat pensive mouth, a cheek pale, thin, and deeply furrowed. A monk fresh from the cloisters of Tintern Abbey, in its proudest days, could scarcely have made a more ascetic and solemn appearance than did Dr. Pusey on this occasion. He is not apparently above forty-five, or at most fifty years of age, and his whole aspect renders him an admirable study for an artist. Dr. Pusey's style of preaching is cold and tame, and one looking at him would scarcely believe that such an apparently uninteresting man could cause such an eruption in the Church as he has. I was glad to find that a coloured young man was among the students at Oxford.

A few months since, I paid a visit to our countryman, Alexander Crummel, who is still pursuing his studies at Cambridge--a place, though much inferior to Oxford as far as appearance is concerned, is yet said to be greatly its superior as a place of learning. In an hour's walk through the Strand, Regent, or Piccadilly Streets in London, one may meet half a dozen coloured young men, who are inmates of the various Colleges in the metropolis. These are all signs of progress in the cause of the sons of Africa. Then let our people take courage, and with that courage let them apply themselves to learning. A determination to excel is the sure road to greatness, and that is as open to the black man as the white. It was that which has accomplished the mightiest and noblest triumphs in the intellectual and physical world. It was that which has made such rapid strides towards civilization, and broken the chains of ignorance and superstition, which have so long fettered the human intellect. It was determination which raised so many worthy individuals from the humble walks of society, and from poverty, and placed them in positions of trust and renown. It is no slight barrier that can effectually oppose the determination of the will--success must ultimately crown its efforts. "The world shall hear of me," was the exclamation of one whose name has become as familiar as household words. A Toussaint, once laboured in the sugar field with his spelling-book in his pocket, amid the combined efforts of a nation to keep him in ignorance. His name is now recorded among the list of statesmen of the past. A Soulouque was once a slave, and knew not how to read. He now sits upon the throne of an Empire.

In our own country, there are men who once held the plough, and that too without any compensation, who are now presiding at the editor's table. It was determination that brought out the genius of a Franklin, and a Fulton, and that has distinguished many of the American Statesmen, who but for their energy and determination would never have had a name beyond the precincts of their own homes.

It is not always those who have the best advantages, or the greatest talents, that eventually succeed in their undertakings; but it is those who strive with untiring diligence to remove all obstacles to success, and who, with unconquerable resolution, labour on until the rich reward of perseverance is within their grasp. Then again let me say to our young men--Take courage; "There is a good time coming." The darkness of the night appears greatest just before the dawn of day.

LETTER XX.

Fugitive Slaves in England.

The love of freedom is one of those natural impulses of the human breast which cannot be extinguished. Even the brute animals of the creation feel and show sorrow and affection when deprived of their liberty. Therefore is a distinguished writer justified in saying, "Man is free, even were he born in chains." The Americans boast, and justly, too, that Washington was the hero and model patriot of the American Revolution--the man whose fame, unequalled in his own day and country, will descend to the end of time, the pride and honour of humanity. The American speaks with pride of the battles of Lexington and Bunker Hill; and when standing in Faneuil Hall, he points to the portraits of Otis, Adams, Hancock, Quincy, Warren, and Franklin, and tells you that their names will go down to posterity among the world's most devoted and patriotic friends of human liberty.

It was on the first of August, 1851, that a number of men, fugitives from that boasted land of freedom, assembled at the Hall of Commerce in the City of London, for the purpose of laying their wrongs before the British nation, and at the same time, to give thanks to the God of

Freedom for the liberation of their West India brethren, on the first of August, 1834. Little notice had been given of the intended meeting, yet it seemed to be known in all parts of the city. At the hour of half-past seven, for which the meeting had been called, the spacious hall was well filled, and the fugitives, followed by some of the most noted English Abolitionists, entered the hall, amid the most deafening applause, and took their seats on the platform. The appearance of the great hall at this juncture was most splendid. Besides the committee of fugitives, on the platform there were a number of the oldest and most devoted of the Slave's friends. On the left of the chair sat Geo. Thompson, Esq., M.P.; near him was the Rev. Jabez Burns, D.D.; and by his side the Rev. John Stevenson, M.A., Wm. Farmer, Esq., R. Smith, Esq.; while on the other side were the Rev. Edward Mathews, John Cunliff, Esq., Andrew Paton, Esq., J.P. Edwards, Esq., and a number of coloured gentlemen from the West Indies. The body of the hall was not without its distinguished guests. The Chapmans and Westons of Boston, U.S., were there. The Estlins and Tribes had come all the way from Bristol to attend the great meeting. The Patons of Glasgow had delayed their departure, so as to be present. The Massies had come in from Upper Clapton. Not far from the platform sat Sir Francis Knowles, Bart., still farther back was Samuel Bowly, Esq., while near the door were to be seen the greatest critic of the age, and England's best living poet. Macaulay had laid aside the pen, entered the hall, and was standing near the central door, while not far from the historian stood the newly-appointed Poet Laureat. The author of "In Memoriam" had been swept in by the crowd, and was standing with his arms folded, and beholding for the first time (and probably the last) so large a number of coloured men in one room. In different parts of the hall were men and women from nearly all parts of the kingdom, besides a large number who, drawn to London by the Exhibition, had come in to see and hear these oppressed people plead their own cause.

The writer of this sketch was chosen Chairman of the meeting, and commenced its proceedings by delivering the following address, which we cut from the columns of the *Morning Advertiser*:--

"The Chairman, in opening the proceedings, remarked that, although the metropolis had of late been inundated with meetings of various character, having reference to almost every variety of subject, yet that the subject they were called upon that evening to discuss differed from them all. Many of those by whom he was surrounded, like himself, had been victims to the inhuman institution of Slavery, and were in consequence exiled from the land of their birth. They were fugitives from their native land, but not fugitives from justice, and they had not fled from a monarchical, but from a so-called republican government. They came from amongst a people who declared, as part of their creed, that all men were born free, but who, while they did so, made slaves of every sixth man, woman, and child in the country (hear, hear). He must not, however, forget that one of the purposes for which they were met that night was to commemorate the emancipation of their brothers and sisters in the isles of the sea. That act of the British Parliament, and he might add in this case with peculiar emphasis, of the British nation, passed on the 12th day of August, 1833, to take effect on the first day of August, 1834, and which enfranchised 800,000 West Indian slaves, was an event sublime in its nature, comprehensive and mighty in its immediate influences and remote consequences, precious beyond expression to the cause of freedom, and encouraging beyond the measure of any government on earth to the hearts of all enlightened and just men. This act was the commencement of a long course of philanthropic and Christian efforts on the part of some of the best men that the world ever produced. It was not his intention to go into a discussion or a calculation of the rise and fall of property, or whether sugar was worth more or less by the act of emancipation. But the abolition of Slavery in the West Indies, was a blow struck in the right direction, at that most inhuman of all traffics, the slave trade--a trade which would never cease so long as slavery existed, for where there was a market there would be merchandise; where there was demand there would be a supply; where there were carcases there would be vultures; and they might as well attempt to turn the water, and make it run up the Niagara river, as to change this law. It was often said by the Americans that England was responsible for the existence of slavery there, because it was introduced into that country while the colonies were under the British Crown. If that were the case, they must come to the conclusion that, as England abolished Slavery in the West Indies, she would have done the same for the American States if she had had the power to do it; and if that was so, they might safely say that the separation of the United States from the mother country was (to say the least) a great misfortune to one-sixth of the population of that land. England had set a noble example to America, and he would to heaven his countrymen would follow the example. The Americans boasted of their superior knowledge, but they needed not to boast of their superior guilt, for that was set upon a hill top, and that too, so high, that it required not the lantern of Diogenes to find it out. Every breeze from the western world brought upon its wings the groans and cries of the victims of this guilt. Nearly all countries had fixed the seal of disapprobation on slavery, and when, at some future age, this stain on the page of history shall be pointed at, posterity will blush at the discrepancy between American profession and American practice. What was to be thought of a people boasting of their liberty, their humanity, their Christianity, their love of justice, and at the same time keeping in slavery nearly four millions of God's children, and shutting out from them the light of the Gospel, by denying the Bible to the slave! (Hear, hear.) No education, no marriage, everything done to keep the mind of the slave in darkness. There was a wish on the part of the people of the northern States to shield themselves from the charge of slave-holding, but as they shared in the guilt, he was not satisfied with letting them off without their share in the odium. And now a word about the Fugitive Slave Bill. That measure was in every respect an unconstitutional measure. It set aside the right formerly enjoyed by the fugitive of trial by jury--it afforded to him no protection, no opportunity of proving his right to be free, and it placed every free coloured person at the mercy of any unprincipled individual who might wish to lay claim to him. (Hear.) That law is opposed to the principles of Christianity--foreign alike to the laws of God and man, it had converted the whole population of the free States into a band of slave-catchers, and every rood of territory is but so much hunting ground, over which they might chase the fugitive. But while they were speaking of slavery in the United States, they must not omit to mention that there was a strong feeling in that land, not only against the Fugitive Slave Law, but also against the existence of slavery in any form. There was a band of fearless men and women in the city of Boston, whose labours for the slave had resulted in good beyond calculation. This noble and heroic class had created an agitation in the whole country, until their principles have taken root in almost every association in the land, and which, with God's blessing, will, in due time, cause the Americans to put into practice what they have so long professed. (Hear, hear.) He wished it to be continually held up before the country, that the northern States are as deeply implicated in the guilt of slavery as the South. The north had a population of 13,553,328 freemen; the south had a population of only 6,393,756 freemen; the north has 152 representatives in the house, the south only 81; and it would be seen by this, that the balance of power was with the free States. Looking, therefore, at the question in all its aspects, he was sure that there was no one in this country but who would find out, that the slavery of the United States of America was a system the most abandoned and the most tyrannical. (Hear, hear.)"

At the close of this address, the Rev. Edward Matthews, last from Bristol, but who had recently returned from the United States, where he had been maltreated on account of his fidelity to the cause of freedom, was introduced, and made a most interesting speech. The next speaker was George Thompson, Esq., M.P.; and we need only say that his eloquence, which has seldom or ever been equalled, and never surpassed, exceeded, on this occasion, the most sanguine expectations of his friends. All who sat under the thundering anathemas which he hurled against slavery, seemed instructed, delighted, and animated. No one could scarcely have remained unmoved by the pensive sympathies that pervaded the entire assembly. There were many in the meeting who had never seen a fugitive slave before, and when any of the speakers would refer to those on the platform, the whole audience seemed moved to tears. No meeting of the kind held in London for years created a greater sensation than this gathering of refugees from the "Land of the free, and the home of the brave." The following appeal, which I had written for the occasion, was unanimously adopted at the close of the meeting, and thus ended the great Anti-Slavery demonstration of 1851.

AN APPEAL TO THE PEOPLE OF GREAT BRITAIN AND THE WORLD.

We consider it just, both to the people of the United States and to ourselves, in making an appeal to the inhabitants of other countries, against the laws which have exiled us from our native land, to state the ground upon which we make our appeal, and the causes which impel us to do so. There are in the United States of America, at the present time, between three and four millions of persons, who are held in a state of slavery which has no parallel in any other part of the world; and whose numbers have, within the last fifty years, increased to a fearful extent. These people are not only deprived of the rights to which the laws of Nature and Nature's God entitle them, but every avenue to knowledge is closed against them. The laws do not recognise the family relation of a slave, and extend to him protection in the enjoyment of domestic endearments. Brothers and sisters, parents and children, husbands and wives, are torn asunder, and permitted to see each other no more. The shrieks and agonies of the slave are heard in the markets at the seat of government, and within hearing of the American Congress, as well as on the cotton, sugar and rice plantations of the far South.

The history of the negroes in America is but a history of repeated injuries and acts of oppression committed upon them by the whites. It is not for ourselves that we make this appeal, but for those whom we have left behind.

In their Declaration of Independence, the Americans declare that "all men are created equal; that they are endowed by their Creator with certain inalienable rights; that among these are life, liberty, and the pursuit of happiness." Yet one-sixth of the inhabitants of the great Republic are slaves. Thus they give the lie to their own professions. No one forfeits his or her character or standing in society by being engaged in holding, buying or selling a slave; the details of which, in all their horror, can scarcely be told.

Although the holding of slaves is confined to fifteen of the thirty-one States, yet we hold that the non-slave-holding States are equally guilty with the slave-holding. If any proof is needed on this point, it will be found in the passage of the inhuman Fugitive Slave Law, by Congress; a law which could never have been enacted without the votes of a portion of the representatives from the free States, and which is now being enforced, in many of the States, with the utmost alacrity. It was the passing of this law that exiled us from our native land, and it has driven thousands of our brothers and sisters from the free States, and compelled them to seek a refuge in the British possessions in North America. The Fugitive Slave Law has converted the entire country, North and South, into one vast hunting-ground. We would respectfully ask you to expostulate with the Americans, and let them know that you regard their treatment of the coloured people of that country as a violation of every principle of human brotherhood, of natural right, of justice, of humanity, of Christianity, of love to God and love to man.

It is needless that we should remind you that the religious sects of

America, with but few exceptions, are connected with the sin of slavery--the churches North as well as South. We would have you tell the professed Christians of that land, that if they would be respected by you, they must separate themselves from the unholy alliance with men who are daily committing deeds which, if done in England, would cause the perpetrator to be sent to a felon's doom; that they must refuse the right hand of Christian fellowship, whether individually or collectively, to those implicated, in any way, in the guilt of slavery.

We do not ask for a forcible interference on your part, but only that you will use all lawful and peaceful means to restore to this much injured race their God-given rights. The moral and religious sentiment of mankind must be arrayed against slave-holding, to make it infamous, ere we can hope to see it abolished. We would ask you to set them the example, by excluding from your pulpits, and from religious communion, the slave-holding and pro-slavery ministers who may happen to visit this country. We would even go further, and ask you to shut your doors against either ministers or laymen, who are at all guilty of upholding and sustaining this monster sin. By the cries of the slave, which come from the fields and swamps of the far South, we ask you to do this! By that spirit of liberty and equality of which you all admire, we would ask you to do this. And by that still nobler, higher, and holier spirit of our beloved Saviour, we would ask you to stamp upon the head of the slaveholder, with a brand deeper than that which marks the victim of his wrongs, the infamy of theft, adultery, man-stealing, piracy, and murder, and, by the force of public opinion, compel him to "unloose the heavy burden, and let the oppressed go free."

LETTER XXI.

A Chapter on American Slavery.

The word Englishman is but another name for an American, and the word American is but another name for an Englishman--England is the father, America the son. They have a common origin and identity of language; they hold the same religious and political opinions; they study the same histories, and have the same literature. Steam and mechanical ingenuity have brought the two countries within nine days sailing of each other. The Englishman on landing at New-York finds his new neighbours speaking the same language which he last heard on leaving Liverpool, and he sees the American in the same dress that he had been accustomed to look upon at home, and soon forgets that he is three thousand miles from his native land, and in another country. The American on landing at Liverpool, and taking a walk through the great commercial city, finding no difficulty in understanding the people, supposes himself still in New-York; and if there seems any doubt in his own mind, growing out of the fact that the people have a more healthy look, seem more polite, and that the buildings have a more substantial appearance than those he had formerly looked upon, he has only to imagine, as did Rip Van Winkle, that he has been asleep these hundred years.

If the Englishman who has seen a Thompson silenced in Boston, or a Macready mobbed in New-York, upon the ground that they were foreigners, should sit in Exeter Hall and hear an American orator until he was hoarse, and wonder why the American is better treated in England than the Englishman in America, he has only to attribute it to John Bull's superior knowledge of good manners, and his being a more law-abiding man than brother Jonathan. England and America has each its reforms and its reformers, and they have more or less sympathy with each other. It has been said that one generation commences a reform in England, and that another generation finishes it. I would that so much could be said with regard to the great object of reform in America--the system of slavery!

No evil was ever more deeply rooted in a country than is slavery in the United States. Spread over the largest and most fertile States in the Union, with decidedly the best climate, and interwoven, as it is, with the religious, political, commercial, and social institutions of the country, it is scarcely possible to estimate its influence. This is the evil which claims the attention of American Reformers, over and above every other evil in the land, and thanks to a kind providence, the American slave is not without his advocates. The greatest enemy to the Anti-Slavery Society, and the most inveterate opposer of the men whose names stand at the head of the list as officers and agents of that association, will, we think, assign to William Lloyd Garrison, the first place in the ranks of the American Abolitionists. The first to proclaim the doctrine of immediate emancipation to the slaves of America, and on that account an object of hatred to the slave-holding interest of the country, and living for years with his life in danger, he is justly regarded by all, as the leader of the Anti-Slavery movement in the New World. Mr. Garrison is at the present time but little more than forty-five years of age, and of the middle size. He has a high and prominent forehead, well developed, with no hair on the top of the head, having lost it in early life; with a piercing eye, a pleasant, yet anxious countenance, and of a most loveable disposition; tender, and blameless in his family affections, devoted to his friends; simple and studious, upright, guileless, distinguished, and worthy, like the distinguished men of antiquity, to be immortalized by another Plutarch. How many services never to be forgotten, has he not rendered to the cause of the slave, and the welfare of mankind! As a speaker, he is forcible, clear, and logical, yet he will not rank with the many who are less known. As a writer, he is regarded as one of the finest in the

United States, and certainly the most prominent in the Anti-Slavery cause. Had Mr. Garrison wished to serve himself, he might, with his great talents, long since, have been at the head of either of the great political parties. Few men can withstand the allurements of office, and the prize-money that accompanies them. Many of those who were with him fifteen years ago, have been swept down with the current of popular favour, either in Church or State. He has seen a Cox on the one hand, and a Stanton on the other, swept away like so much floating wood before the tide. When the sturdiest characters gave way, when the finest geniuses passed one after another under the yoke of slavery, Garrison stood firm to his convictions, like a rock that stands stirless amid the conflicting agitation of the waves. He is not only the friend and advocate of freedom with his pen and his tongue, but to the oppressed of every clime he opens his purse, his house, and his heart: yet he is not a man of money. The fugitive slave, fresh from the whips and chains, who is turned off by the politician, and experiences the cold shoulder of the divine, finds a bed and a breakfast under the hospitable roof of Mr. Lloyd Garrison.

The party of which he is the acknowledged head, is one of no inconsiderable influence in the United States. No man has more bitter enemies or stauncher friends than he. There are those among his friends who would stake their all upon his veracity and integrity; and we are sure that the coloured people throughout America, bond and free, in whose cause he has so long laboured, will, with one accord, assign the highest niche in their affection to the champion of universal emancipation. Every cause has its writers and its orators. We have drawn a hasty and imperfect sketch of the greatest writer in the Anti-Slavery field: we shall now call attention to the most distinguished public speaker. The name of Wendell Phillips is but another name for eloquence. Born in the highest possible position in America, Mr. Phillips has all the advantages that birth can give to one in that country. Educated at the first University, graduating with all the honours which the College could bestow on him, and studying the law and becoming a member of the bar, he has all the accomplishments that these advantages can give to a man of a great mind. Nature has treated him as a favourite. His stature is not tall, but handsome; his expressive countenance paints and reflects every emotion of his soul. His gestures are wonderfully graceful, like his delivery. There is a fascination in the soft gaze of his eyes, which none can but admire. Being a great reader, and endowed by nature with a good memory, he supplies himself with the most complicated dates and historical events. Nothing can equal the variety of his matter. I have heard him more than twenty different times on the same subject, but never heard the same speech. He is personal, but there is nothing offensive in his personalities. He extracts from a subject all that it contains, and does it as none but Wendell Phillips can. His voice is beautifully musical, and it is calculated to attract wherever it is heard. He is a man of calm intrepidity, of a patriotic and warm heart, with manners the most affable, temper the most gentle, a rectitude of principle entirely natural, a freedom from ambition, and a modesty quite singular. As Napoleon kept the Old Guard in reserve, to turn the tide in battle, so do the Abolitionists keep Mr. Phillips in reserve when opposition is expected in their great gatherings. We have seen the meetings turned into a bedlam, by the mobocratic slave-holding spirit, and when the speakers had one after another left the platform without a hearing, and the chairman had lost all control of the assembly, the appearance of this gentleman upon the platform would turn the tide of events. He would not beg for a hearing, but on the contrary, he would lash them as no preceding speaker had done. If, by their groans and yells, they stifled his voice, he would stand unmoved with his arms folded, and by the very eloquence of his looks put them to silence. His speeches against the Fugitive Slave Law, and his withering rebukes of Daniel Webster and other northern men who supported that measure, are of the most splendid character, and will compare in point of composition with anything ever uttered by Chatham or Sheridan in their palmiest days. As a public speaker, Mr. Phillips is, without doubt, the first in the United States. Considering his great talent, his high birth, and the prospects which lay before him, and the fact that he threw everything aside to plead the slave's cause, we must be convinced that no man has sacrificed more upon the altar of humanity than Wendell Phillips.

Within the past ten years, a great impetus has been given to the anti-slavery movement in America by coloured men who have escaped from slavery. Coming as they did from the very house of bondage, and being able to speak from sad experience, they could speak as none others could.

The gentleman to whom we shall now call attention is one of this class, and doubtless the first of his race in America. The name of Frederick Douglass is well known throughout this country as well as America. Born and brought up as a slave, he was deprived of a mother's care and of early education. Escaping when he was little more than twenty years of age, he was thrown upon his own resources in the free states, where prejudice against colour is but another name for slavery. But during all this time he was educating himself as well as circumstances would admit. Mr. Douglass commenced his career as a public speaker some ten years since, as an agent of the American or Massachusetts Anti-Slavery Societies. He is tall and well made. His vast and well-developed forehead announces the power of his intellect. His voice is full and sonorous. His attitude is dignified, and his gesticulation is full of noble simplicity. He is a man of lofty reason, natural, and without pretension, always master of himself, brilliant in the art of exposing and of abstracting. Few persons can handle a subject with which they are familiar better than Mr. Douglass. There is a kind of eloquence issuing from the depth of the soul, as from a spring, rolling along its copious floods, sweeping all before it, overwhelming by its very force, carrying, upsetting, engulphing its adversaries, and more dazzling and more thundering than the bolt which leaps from crag to crag. This is the eloquence of Frederick Douglass. He is one of the greatest mimics of the age. No man can put on a sweeter smile or a more sarcastic frown than he: you cannot put him off his guard. He is always in good humour. Mr. Douglass possesses great dramatic powers; and had he taken up the sock and buskin, instead of becoming a lecturer, he would have made as fine a Coriolanus as ever trod the stage.

However, Mr. Douglass was not the first coloured man that became a lecturer, and thereby did service to the cause of his countrymen. The earliest and most effective speaker from among the coloured race in America, was Charles Lennox Remond. In point of eloquence, this gentleman is not inferior to either Wendell Phillips or Frederick Douglass. Mr. Remond is of small stature, and neat figure, with a head well developed, but a remarkably thin face. As an elocutionist, he is, without doubt, the first on the anti-slavery platform. He has a good voice, a pleasing countenance, a prompt intelligence, and when speaking, is calculated to captivate and carry away an audience by the very force of his eloquence. Born in the freest state of the Union, and of most respectable parents, he prides himself not a little on his birth and descent. One can scarcely find fault with this, for, in the United States, the coloured man is deprived of the advantages which parentage gives to the white man. Mr. Remond is a descendant of one of those coloured men who stood side by side with white men on the plains of Concord and Lexington, in the battles that achieved the independence of the colonies from the mother country, in the war of the Revolution. Mr. Remond has felt deeply, (probably more so than any other coloured man), the odious prejudice against colour. On this point he is sensitive to a fault. If any one will sit for an hour and hear a lecture from him on this subject, if he is not converted, he will at least become convinced, that the boiling cauldron of anti-slavery discussion has never thrown upon its surface a more fiery spirit than Charles Lennox Remond.

There are some men who neither speak nor write, but whose lives place them in the foremost ranks in the cause which they espouse. One of these is Francis Jackson. He was one of the earliest to give countenance and support to the anti-slavery movement. In the year 1835, when a mob of more than 5000 merchants and others, in Boston, broke up an anti-slavery meeting of females, at which William Lloyd Garrison and George Thompson were to deliver addresses, and when the Society had no room in which to hold its meetings (having been driven from their own room by the mob), Francis Jackson, with a moral courage scarcely ever equalled, came forward and offered his private dwelling to the ladies, to hold their meeting in. The following interesting passage occurs in a letter from him to the Secretary of the Society a short time after, on receiving a vote of thanks from its members:--

"If a large majority of this community choose to turn a deaf ear to the wrongs which are inflicted upon their countrymen in other portions of the land--if they are content to turn away from the sight of oppression, and 'pass by on the other side'--so it must be.

"But when they undertake in any way to impair or annul my right to speak, write, and publish upon any subject, and more especially upon enormities, which are the common concern of every lover of his country and his kind--so it must not be--so it shall not be, if I for one can prevent it. Upon this great right let us hold on at all hazards. And should we, in its exercise, be driven from public halls to private dwellings, one house at least shall be consecrated to its preservation. And if, in defence of this sacred privilege, which man did not give me, and shall not (if I can help it) take from me, this roof and these walls shall be levelled to the earth, let them fall if they must; they cannot crumble in a better cause. They will appear of very little value to me after their owner shall have been whipt into silence."

There are among the contributors to the Anti-Slavery cause, a few who give with a liberality which has never been surpassed by the donors to any benevolent association in the world, according to their means--the chief of these is Francis Jackson.

In the month of May, 1844, while one evening strolling up Broadway, New York, I saw a crowd making its way into the Minerva Rooms, and, having no pressing engagement, I followed, and was soon in a splendid hall, where some twelve or fifteen hundred persons were seated, and listening to rather a strange-looking man. The speaker was tall and slim, with long arms, long legs, and a profusion of auburn or reddish hair hanging in ringlets down his shoulders; while a huge beard of the same colour fell upon his breast. His person was not at all improved by his dress. The legs of his trousers were shorter than those worn by smaller men: the sleeves of his coat were small and short, the shirt collar turned down in Byronic style, beard and hair hid his countenance, so that no redeeming feature could be found there; yet there was one redeeming quality about the man--that was the stream of fervid eloquence which escaped from his lips. I inquired his name, and was informed that it was Charles C. Burleigh. Nature has been profuse in showering her gifts upon Mr. Burleigh, but all has been bestowed upon his head and heart. There is a kind of eloquence which weaves its thread around the hearer, and gradually draws him into its web, fascinating him with its gaze, entangling him as the spider does the fly, until he is fast: such is the eloquence of C.C. Burleigh. As a debater he is unquestionably the first on the Anti-slavery platform. If he did not speak so fast, he would equal Wendell Phillips; if he did not reason his subject out of existence, he would surpass him. However, one would have to travel over many miles, and look in the faces of many men, before he would find one who has made more personal sacrifices, or done more to bring about the Emancipation of the American Slaves, than Mr. Charles C. Burleigh.

Whoever the future historian of the Anti-Slavery movement may be, he will not be able to compile a correct history of this great struggle, without consulting the writings of Edmund Quincy, a member of one of the wealthiest, patriotic, and aristocratic families in New England: the prestige of his name is a passport to all that the heart could wish. Descended from a family, whose name is connected with all that was glorious in the great American Revolution, the son of one who has again and again represented his native State, in the National Congress, he too, like Wendell Phillips, threw away the pearl of political preferment, and devoted his distinguished talents to the cause of the Slave. Mr. Quincy is better known in this country as having filled the editorial chair of *The Liberator*, during the several visits of its Editor to Great Britain. As a speaker, he does not rank as high as some who are less known; as a writer, he has few equals. The "Annual Reports" of the American and Massachusetts Anti-Slavery Societies for the past fifteen or twenty years, have emanated from his pen. When posterity, in digging among the tombs of the friends of mankind, and of universal freedom, shall fail to find there the name of Edmund Quincy, it will be because the engraver failed to do his duty.

Were we sent out to find a man who should excel all others in collecting together new facts and anecdotes, and varnishing up old ones so that they would appear new, and bringing them into a meeting and emptying out, good or bad, the whole contents of his sack, to the delight and admiration of the audience, we would unhesitatingly select James N. Buffum as the man. If Mr. Buffum is not a great speaker, he has what many accomplished orators have not--*i.e.*, a noble and generous heart. If the fugitive slave, fresh from the cotton-field, should make his appearance in the town of Lynn, in Massachusetts, and should need a night's lodging or refreshments, he need go no farther than the hospitable door of James N. Buffum.

Most men who inherit large fortunes, do little or nothing to benefit mankind. A few, however, spend their means in the best possible manner: one of the latter class is Gerrit Smith. The name of this gentleman should have been brought forward among those who are first mentioned in this chapter. Some eight or ten years ago, Mr. Smith was the owner of large tracts of land, lying in twenty-nine counties in the State of New York, and came to the strange conclusion to give the most of it away. Consequently, three thousand lots of land, containing from thirty to one hundred acres each, were given to coloured men residing in the State--the writer of this being one of the number.

Although universal suffrage is enjoyed by the whites in the State of New York, a property-qualification is imposed on coloured men; and this act of Mr. Smith's not only made three thousand men the owners of land, but created also three thousand voters. The ability to give, and the willingness to do so, is not by any means the greatest quality of this gentleman. As a public speaker, Mr. Smith has few equals; and certainly no man in his State has done more to forward the cause of Negro Emancipation than he.

We have already swelled the pages of this chapter beyond what we intended when we commenced, but yet we have called attention to only one branch of American Reformers. The Temperance Reformers are next to be considered. This cause has many champions, and yet none who occupy a very prominent position before the world. The first temperance newspaper published in the United States, was edited by William Lloyd Garrison. Gerrit Smith has also done much in promulgating temperance views. But the most noted man in the movement at the present time, and the one best known to the British public, is John B. Gough. This gentleman was at one time an actor on the stage, and subsequently became an inebriate of the most degraded kind. He was, however, reclaimed through the great Washingtonian movement that swept over the United States a few years since. In stature, Mr. Gough is tall and slim, with black hair, which he usually wears too long. As an orator, he is considered among the first in the United States. Having once been an actor, he throws all his dramatic powers into his addresses. He has a facility of telling strange and marvellous stories which can scarcely be surpassed; and what makes them still more interesting, he always happens to be an eyewitness. While speaking, he acts the drunkard, and does it in a style which could not be equalled on the boards of the Lyceum or Adelphi. No man has obtained more signatures to the temperance pledge than he. After all, it is a question whether he has ever been of any permanent service to this reform or not. Mr. Gough has more than once fallen from his position as a teetotaler; more than once he has broken his pledge, and when found by his friends, was in houses of a questionable character. However, some are of opinion that these defects have been of use to him; for when he has made his appearance after one of these debaucheries, the people appear to sympathize more with him, and some thought he spoke better. If we believe that a person could enjoy good health with water upon the brain, we would be of opinion that Mr. Gough's cranium contained a greater quantity than that of any other living man. When speaking before an audience, he can weep when he pleases; and the tears shed on these occasions are none of your make-believe kind--none of your small drops trickling down the cheeks one at a time;--but they come in great showers, so as even to sprinkle upon the paper which he holds in his hand. Of course, he is not alone in shedding tears in his meetings, many of his hearers usually join him; especially the ladies, as these showers are intended for them. However, no one can sit for an hour and hear John. B. Gough, without coming to the conclusion that he is nothing more than a theatrical mountebank.

The ablest speaker on the subject of Peace, is Charles Sumner. Standing more than six feet in height, and well proportioned, Mr. Sumner makes a most splendid and commanding appearance before an assembly. It is not his looks alone that attract attention--his very countenance indicates a superior mind. Born in the upper circle, educated in the first College in the country, and finally becoming a member of the Bar, he is well qualified to take the highest possible position as a public speaker. As an orator, Charles Sumner has but one superior in the United States, and that is Wendell Phillips. Mr. Sumner is an able advocate for the liberation of the American Slaves as well as of the cause of Peace, and has rendered great aid to the abolition movement.

The name of Elihu Burritt, for many reasons, should be placed at the head of the Peace Movement. No man was ever more devoted to one idea than he is to that of peace. If he is an advocate of Temperance, it is because it will promote peace. If he opposes Slavery, it is upon the grounds of peace. Ask him why he wants an "Ocean Penny Postage," he will tell you to engender the principles of peace. Everything with him hinges upon the doctrine of peace. As a speaker, Mr. Burritt does not rank amongst the first. However, his speeches are of a high order, some think them too high, and complain that he is too much of a cloud-traveller, and when he descends from these aerial flights and cloudy thrones, they are unwilling to admit that he can be practical. If Mr. Burritt should prove as good a statesman as a theorist, he would be an exception to most who belong to the aerial school. As a writer he stands deservedly high. In his "Sparks from the Anvil," and "Voice from the Forge," are to be found as fine pieces as have been produced by any writer of the day. His "Drunkard's Wife" is the most splendid thing of the kind in the language. His stature is of the middle size, head well developed, with eyes deeply set, and a prepossessing countenance, though not handsome; he wears an exterior of remarkable austerity, and everything about him is grave, even to his smile. Being well versed in the languages, ancient and modern, he does not lack variety or imagination, either in his public addresses or private conversation; yet it would be difficult to find a man with a better heart, or sweeter spirit, than Elihu Burritt.

LETTER XXII.

A Narrative of American Slavery.

Although the first slaves, introduced into the American Colonies from the coast of Africa, were negroes of a very dark complexion with woolly hair, and it was thought that slavery would be confined to the blacks, yet the present slave population of America is far from being black. This change in colour, is attributable, solely to the unlimited power which the slave owner exercises over his victim. There being no lawful marriage amongst slaves, and no encouragement to slave women to be virtuous and chaste, there seems to be no limits to the system of amalgamation carried on between master and slave. This accounts for the fact, that most persons who go from Europe, or from the Free States, into Carolina or Virginia, are struck with the different shades of colour amongst the slaves. On a plantation employing fifty slaves, it is not uncommon to see one third of them mulattoes, and some of these nearly white.

In the year 1831, there resided in the state of Virginia, a slave who was so white, that no one would suppose for a moment that a drop of African blood coursed through his veins. His skin was fair, hair soft, straight, fine and white; his eyes blue, nose prominent, lips thin; his head well formed, forehead high and prominent; and he was often taken for a white free person, by those who did not know him. This made his condition as a slave still more intolerable; for one so white, seldom ever receives fair treatment at the hands of his fellow slaves; and the whites usually regard such slaves as persons, who, if not often flogged and otherwise ill treated, to remind them of their condition, would soon "forget" that they were slaves, and "think themselves as good as white folks." During that year, an insurrection broke out amongst the slave population, known as the Southampton Rebellion, or the "Nat Turner Insurrection." Five or six hundred slaves, believing in the doctrine that "all men are created equal," armed with such weapons as they could get, commenced a war for freedom. Amongst these was George, the white slave of whom we have spoken. He had been employed as a house servant, and had heard his master and visiters speak of the down-trodden and oppressed Poles; he heard them talk of going to Greece to fight for Grecian liberty, and against the oppressors of that ill-fated people. George, fired with the love of freedom, and zeal for the cause of his enslaved countrymen, joined the insurrection. The result of that struggle for liberty is well known. The slaves were defeated, and those who were not taken prisoners, took refuge in the dismal swamps. These were ordered to surrender; but instead of doing so, they challenged their proud oppressors to take them, and immediately renewed the war. A ferocious struggle now commenced between the parties; but not until the United States troops were called in, did they succeed in crushing a handful of men and women who were fighting for freedom. The negroes were hunted with dogs, and many who were caught were burnt alive; while some were hung, and others flogged and banished from the State.

Among those who were sentenced to be hanged, was George. He was placed in prison to await the day of execution, which would give him ten days to prepare for his doom. George was the son of a member of the American Congress, his mother being a servant in the principal hotel in Washington, where members of Congress usually put up. After the birth of George, his mother was sold to a negro trader, and he to a Virginian, who sent agents through the country to buy up young slaves to raise for the market. George was only about nineteen years of age, when he unfortunately became connected with the insurrection. Mr. Green, who owned George, was a comparatively good master, and prided himself on treating his slaves better than most men. This gentleman was also the owner of a girl who was perfectly white, with straight hair and prominent features. This girl was said to be the daughter of her own master. A feeling of attachment sprang up between Mary and George, which proved to be more than mere friendship, and upon which we base the burden of this narrative.

After poor George had been sentenced to death and cast into prison, Mary begged and obtained leave to visit George, and administer to him the comforts of religion, as she was a member of a religious body, while George was not. As George had been a considerable favourite with Mrs. Green, Mary had no difficulty in obtaining permission to pay a daily visit to him, to whom she had pledged her heart and hand. At one of these meetings, and only four days from the time fixed for the execution, while Mary was seated in George's cell, it occurred to her that she might yet save him from a felon's doom. She revealed to him the secret that was then occupying her thoughts, viz., that George should exchange clothes with her, and thus attempt his escape in disguise. But he would not for a single moment listen to the proposition. Not that he feared detection; but he would not consent to place an innocent and affectionate girl in a position where she might have to suffer for him. Mary pleaded, but in vain--George was inflexible. The poor girl left her lover with a heavy heart, regretting that her scheme had proved unsuccessful.

Towards the close of the next day, Mary again appeared at the prison door for admission, and was soon by the side of him whom she so ardently loved. While there, the clouds which had overhung the city for some hours, broke, and the rain fell in torrents amid the most terrific thunder and lightning. In the most persuasive manner possible, Mary again importuned George to avail himself of her assistance to escape from an ignominious death. After assuring him that she not being the person condemned, would not receive any injury, he at last consented, and they began to exchange apparel. As George was of small stature, and both were white, there was no difficulty in his passing out without detection: and as she usually left the cell weeping, with handkerchief in hand, and sometimes at her face, he had only to adopt this mode and his escape was safe. They had kissed each other, and Mary had told George where he would find a small parcel of provisions which she had placed in a secluded spot, when the prison-keeper opened the door, and said, "Come, girl, it is time for you to go." George again embraced Mary, and passed out of the gaol. It was already dark and the street lamps were lighted, so that our hero in his new dress had no dread of detection. The provisions were sought out and found, and poor George was soon on the road towards Canada. But neither of them had once thought of a change of dress for George when he should have escaped, and he had walked but a short distance before he felt that a change of his apparel would facilitate his progress. But he dared not go amongst even his coloured associates for fear of being betrayed. However, he made the best of his way on towards Canada, hiding in the woods during the day, and travelling by the guidance of the North Star at night.

One morning, George arrived on the banks of the Ohio river, and found his journey had terminated, unless he could get some one to take him across the river in a secret manner, for he would not be permitted to cross in any of the ferry boats; it being a penalty for crossing a slave, besides the value of the slave. He concealed himself in the tall grass and weeds near the river, to see if he could embrace an opportunity to cross. He had been in his hiding-place but a short time, when he observed a man in a small boat, floating near the shore, evidently fishing. His first impulse was to call out to the man and ask him to take him over to the Ohio side, but the fear that the man was a slaveholder, or one who might possibly arrest him, deterred him from it. The man after rowing and floating about for some time fastened the boat to the root of a tree, and started to a neighbouring farm-house. This was George's moment, and he seized it. Running down the bank, he unfastened the boat, jumped in, and with all the expertness of one accustomed to a boat, rowed across the river and landed on the Ohio side.

Being now in a free state, he thought he might with perfect safety travel on towards Canada. He had, however, gone but a few miles, when he discovered two men on horseback coming behind him. He felt sure that they could not be in pursuit of him, yet he did not wish to be seen by them, so he turned into another road, leading to a house near by. The men followed, and were but a short distance from George, when he ran up to a farm house, before which was standing a farmer-looking man, in a broad-brimmed hat and straight collared coat, whom he implored to save him from the "slave-catchers." The farmer told him to go into the barn near by; he entered by the front door, the farmer following, and closing the door behind George, but remaining outside, and gave directions to his hired man as to what should be done with George. The slaveholders by this time had dismounted, and were in the front of the barn demanding admittance, and charging the farmer with secreting their slave woman, for George was still in the dress of a woman. The Friend, for the farmer proved to be a member of the Society of Friends, told the slave-owners that if they wished to search his barn, they must first get an officer and a search warrant. While the parties were disputing, the farmer began nailing up the front door, and the hired man served the back door in the same way. The slaveholders, finding that they could not prevail on the Friend to allow them to get the slave, determined to go in search of an officer. One was left to see that the slave did not escape from the barn, while the other went off at full speed to Mount Pleasant, the nearest town. George was not the slave of either of these men, nor were they in pursuit of him, but they had lost a woman who had been seen in that vicinity, and when they saw poor George in the disguise of a female, and attempting to elude pursuit, they felt sure they were close upon their victim. However, if they had caught him, although he was not their slave, they would have taken him back and placed him in goal, and there he would have remained until his owner arrived.

After an absence of nearly two hours, the slave owner returned with an officer and found the Friend still driving large nails into the door. In a triumphant tone, and with a corresponding gesture, he handed the search-warrant to the Friend, and said, "There, Sir, now I will see if I can't get my Nigger." "Well," said the Friend, "thou hast gone to work according to law, and thou can now go into my barn." "Lend me your hammer that I may get the door open," said the slaveholder. "Let me see the warrant again." And after reading it over once more, he said, "I see nothing in this paper which says I must supply thee with tools to open my door; if thou wishes to go in, thou must get a hammer elsewhere." The sheriff said, "I will go to a neighbouring farm and borrow something which will introduce us to Miss Dinah;" and he immediately went in search of tools. In a short time the officer returned, and they commenced an assault and battery upon the barn door, which soon yielded; and in went the slaveholder and officer, and began turning up the hay and using all other means to find the lost property; but, to their astonishment, the slave was not there. After all hope of getting Dinah was gone, the slave-owner in a rage, said to the Friend, "My Nigger is not here." "I did not tell thee there was any one here." "Yes, but I saw her go in, and you shut the door behind her, and if she was not in the barn, what did you nail the door for?" "Can't I do what I please with my own barn door? Now I will tell thee; thou need trouble thyself no more, for the person thou art after entered the front door and went out at the back door, and is a long way from here by this time. Thou and thy friend must be somewhat fatigued by this time, wont thou go in and take a little dinner with me?" We need not say that this cool invitation of the good Quaker was not accepted by the slaveholders. George, in the meantime, had been taken to a Friend's dwelling some miles away, where, after laying aside his female attire, and being snugly dressed up in a straight collared coat, and pantaloons to match, was again put on the right road towards Canada. Two weeks after this found him in the town of St. Catharines, working on the farm of Colonel Strut, and attending a night school.

George, however, did not forget his promise to use all means in his power to get Mary out of slavery. He, therefore, laboured with all his might, to obtain money with which to employ some one to go back to Virginia for Mary. After nearly six months' labour at St. Catharines, he employed an English missionary to go and see if the girl could be purchased, and at what price. The missionary went accordingly, but returned with the sad intelligence that on account of Mary's aiding George to escape, the court had compelled Mr. Green to sell her out of the State, and she had been sold to a Negro trader and taken to the New Orleans market. As all hope of getting the girl was now gone, George resolved to quit the American continent for ever. He immediately took passage in a vessel laden with timber, bound for Liverpool, and in five weeks from that time he was standing on the quay of the great English seaport. With little or no education, he found many difficulties in the way of getting a respectable living. However, he obtained a situation as porter in a large house in Manchester, where he worked during the day, and took private lessons at night. In this way he laboured for three years, and was then raised to the situation of a clerk. George was so white as easily to pass for a white man, and being somewhat ashamed of his African descent, he never once mentioned the fact of his having been a slave. He soon became a partner in the firm that employed him, and was now on the road to wealth.

In the year 1842, just ten years after George Green (for he adopted his master's name) arrived in England, he visited France, and spent some days at Dunkirk. It was towards sunset, on a warm day in the month of October, that Mr. Green, after strolling some distance from the Hotel de Leon, entered a burial ground and wandered long alone among the silent dead, gazing upon the many green graves and marble tombstones of those who once moved on the theatre of busy life, and whose sounds of gaiety once fell upon the ear of man. All nature around was hushed in silence, and seemed to partake of the general melancholy which hung over the quiet resting place of departed mortals. After tracing the varied inscriptions which told the characters or conditions of the departed, and viewing the mounds 'neath which the dust of mortality slumbered, he had now reached a secluded spot, near to where an aged weeping willow bowed its thick foliage to the ground, as though anxious to hide from the scrutinizing gaze of curiosity the grave beneath it. Mr. Green seated himself upon a marble tomb, and began to read Roscoe's Leo X., a copy of which he had under his arm. It was then about twilight, and he had scarcely gone through half a page, when he observed a lady in black, leading a boy some five years old up one of the paths; and as the lady's black veil was over her face, he felt somewhat at liberty to eye her more closely. While looking at her, the lady gave a scream and appeared to be in a fainting position, when Mr. Green sprang from his seat in time to save her from falling to the ground. At this moment, an elderly gentleman was seen approaching with a rapid step, who from his appearance was evidently the lady's father, or one intimately connected with her. He came up, and in a confused manner, asked what was the matter. Mr. Green explained as well as he could. After taking up the smelling bottle which had fallen from her hand, and holding it a short time to her face, she soon began to revive. During all this time, the lady's veil had so covered her face, that Mr. Green had not seen it. When she had so far recovered as to be able to raise her head, she again screamed, and fell back into the arms of the old man. It now appeared quite certain, that either the countenance of George Green, or some other object, was the cause of these fits of fainting; and the old gentleman, thinking it was the former, in rather a petulant tone said, "I will thank you, Sir, if you will leave us alone." The child whom the lady was leading had now set up a squall; and amid the death-like appearance of the lady, the harsh look of the old man, and the cries of the boy, Mr. Green left the grounds and returned to his hotel.

Whilst seated by the window, and looking out upon the crowded street, with every now and then the strange scene in the grave-yard vividly before him, Mr. Green thought of the book he had been reading, and, remembering that he had left it on the tomb, where he had suddenly dropped it when called to the assistance of the lady, he immediately determined to return in search of it. After a walk of some twenty minutes, he was again over the spot where he had been an hour before, and from which he had been so unceremoniously expelled by the old man. He looked in vain for the book; it was no where to be found: nothing save a bouquet which the lady had dropped, and which lay half-buried in the grass from having been trodden upon, indicated that any one had been there that evening. Mr. Green took up the bunch of flowers, and again returned to the hotel.

After passing a sleepless night, and hearing the clock strike six, he dropped into a sweet sleep, from which he did not awake until roused by the rap of a servant, who, entering his room, handed him a note which ran as follows:--"Sir,--I owe you an apology for the inconveniences to which you were subjected last evening, and if you will honour us with your presence to dinner to-day at four o'clock, I shall be most happy to give you due satisfaction. My servant will be in waiting for you at half-past three. I am, sir, your obedt. servant, J. Devenant. October 23, to George Green, Esq."

The servant who handed this note to Mr. Green, informed him that the bearer was waiting for a reply. He immediately resolved to accept the invitation, and replied accordingly. Who this person was, and how his name and the hotel where he was stopping had been found out, was indeed a mystery. However, he waited impatiently for the hour when he was to see this new acquaintance, and get the mysterious meeting in the grave-yard solved.

The clock on a neighbouring church had scarcely ceased striking three, when the servant announced that a carriage had called for Mr. Green. In less than half an hour, he was seated in a most sumptuous barouch, drawn by two beautiful iron greys, and rolling along over a splendid gravel road, completely shaded by large trees which appeared to have been the accumulating growth of many centuries. The carriage soon stopped in front of a low villa, and this too was imbedded in magnificent trees covered with moss. Mr. Green alighted and was shown into a superb drawing room, the walls of which were hung with fine specimens from the hands of the great Italian painters, and one by a German artist representing a beautiful monkish legend connected with "The Holy Catherine," and illustrious lady of Alexandria. The furniture had an antique and dignified appearance. High backed chairs stood around the room; a venerable mirror stood on the mantle-shelf; rich curtains of crimson damask hung in folds at either side of the large windows; and a rich Turkey carpet covered the floor. In the centre stood a table covered with books, in the midst of which was an old fashioned vase filled with fresh flowers, whose fragrance was exceedingly pleasant. A faint light, together with the quietness of the hour gave beauty beyond description to the whole scene.

Mr. Green had scarcely seated himself upon the sofa, when the elderly gentleman whom he had met the previous evening made his appearance, followed by the little boy, and introduced himself as Mr. Devenant. A moment more, and a lady--a beautiful brunette--dressed in black, with long curls of a chesnut colour hanging down her cheeks, entered the room. Her eyes were of a dark hazel, and her whole appearance indicated that she was a native of a southern clime. The door at which she entered was opposite to where the two gentlemen were seated. They immediately rose; and Mr. Devenant was in the act of introducing her to Mr. Green, when he observed that the latter had sunk back upon the sofa, and the last word that he remembered to have heard was, "It is her." After this, all was dark and dreamy: how long he remained in this condition it was for another to tell. When he awoke, he found himself stretched upon the sofa, with his boots off, his neckerchief removed, shirt collar unbuttoned, and his head resting upon a pillow. By his side sat the old man, with the smelling bottle in the one hand, and a glass of water in the other, and the little boy standing at the foot of the sofa. As soon as Mr. Green had so far recovered as to be able to speak, he said, "Where am I, and what does this mean?" "Wait a while," replied the old man, "and I will tell you all." After the lapse of some ten minutes he rose from the sofa, adjusted his apparel, and said, "I am now ready to hear anything you have to say." "You were born in America," said the old man. "Yes," he replied. "And you were acquainted with a girl named Mary," continued the old man. "Yes, and I loved her as I can love none other." "The lady whom you met so mysteriously last evening is Mary," replied Mr. Devenant. George Green was silent, but the fountains of mingled grief and joy stole out from beneath his eye lashes, and glistened like pearls upon his pale and marble-like cheeks. At this juncture the lady again entered the room. Mr. Green sprang from the sofa, and they fell into each other's arms, to the surprise of the old man and little George, and to the amusement of the servants who had crept up one by one, and were hid behind the doors or loitering in the hall. When they had given vent to their feelings, they resumed their seats and each in turn related the adventures through which they had passed. "How did you find out my name and address," asked Mr. Green? "After you had left us in the grave-yard, our little George said, 'O, mamma, if there aint a book!' and picked it up and brought it to us. Papa opened it, and said 'the gentleman's name is written in it, and here is a card of the Hotel de Leon, where I suppose he is stopping.' Papa wished to leave the book, and said it was all a fancy of mine that I had ever seen you before, but I was perfectly convinced that you were my own George Green. Are you married?" "No, I am not." "Then, thank God!" exclaimed Mrs. Devenant. The old man who had been silent all this time, said, "Now, Sir, I must apologize for the trouble you were put to last evening." "And you are single now." "Yes," she replied. "This is indeed the Lord's doings," said Mr. Green, at the same time bursting into a flood of tears. Although Mr. Devenant was past the age when men should think upon matrimonial subjects, yet this scene brought vividly before his eyes the days when he was a young man, and had a wife living, and he thought it time to call their attention to dinner, which was then waiting. We need scarcely add, that Mr. Green and Mrs. Devenant did very little towards diminishing the dinner that day.

After dinner the lovers (for such we have to call them) gave their experience from the time that George Green left the gaol, dressed in Mary's clothes. Up to that time, Mr. Green's was substantially as we have related it. Mrs. Devenant's was as follows:--"The night after you left the prison," said she, "I did not shut my eyes in sleep. The next morning, about 8 o'clock, Peter, the gardener, came to the gaol to see if I had been there the night before, and was informed that I had, and that I left a little after dark. About an hour after, Mr. Green came himself, and I need not say that he was much surprised on finding me there, dressed in your clothes. This was the first tidings they had of your escape." "What did Mr. Green say when he found that I had fled?" "O!" continued Mrs. Devenant, "he said to me when no one was near, I hope George will get off, but I fear you will have to suffer in his stead. I told him that if it must be so I was willing to die if you could live." At this moment George Green burst into tears, threw his arms around her neck, and exclaimed, "I am glad I have waited so long, with the hope of meeting you again."

Mrs. Devenant again resumed her story:--"I was kept in gaol three days, during which time I was visited by the Magistrates and two of the Judges. On the third day I was taken out, and master told me that I was liberated, upon condition that I be immediately sent out of the State. There happened to be just at that time in the neighbourhood a negro-trader, and he purchased me, and I was taken to New Orleans. On the steam-boat we were kept in a close room where slaves are usually confined, so that I saw nothing of the passengers on board or the towns we passed. We arrived at New Orleans and were all put into the slave-market for sale. I was examined by many persons, but none seemed willing to purchase me; as all thought me too white, and said I would run away and pass as a free white woman. On the second day while in the slave-market, and while planters and others were examining slaves and making their purchases, I observed a tall young man with long black hair eyeing me very closely, and then talking to the trader. I felt sure that my time had now come, but the day closed without my being sold. I did not regret this, for I had heard that foreigners made the worst of masters, and I felt confident that the man who eyed me so closely was not an American.

"The next day was the Sabbath. The bells called the people to the different places of worship. Methodists sang, and Baptists immersed, and Presbyterians sprinkled, and Episcopalians read their prayers, while the ministers of the various sects preached that Christ died for all; yet there were some twenty-five or thirty of us poor creatures confined in the '*Negro Pen*' awaiting the close of the Holy Sabbath, and the dawn of another day, to be again taken into the market, there to be examined like so many beasts of burden. I need not tell you with what anxiety we waited for the advent of another day. On Monday we were again brought out, and placed in rows to be inspected; and fortunately for me, I was sold before we had been on the stand an hour. I was purchased by a gentleman residing in the city, for a waiting-maid for his wife, who was just on the eve of starting for Mobile, to pay a visit to a near relation. I was then dressed to suit the situation of a maid-servant; and, upon the whole, I thought that in my new dress I looked as much the lady as my mistress.

"On the passage to Mobile, who should I see among the passengers, but the tall, long-haired man that had eyed me so closely in the slave-market a few days before. His eyes were again on me, and he appeared anxious to speak to me, and I as reluctant to be spoken to. The first evening after leaving New Orleans, soon after twilight had let her curtain down, and pinned it with a star, and while I was seated on the deck of the boat, near the ladies' cabin, looking upon the rippled waves, and the reflection of the moon upon the sea, all at once I saw the tall young man standing by my side. I immediately rose from my seat, and was in the act of returning to the cabin, when he in a broken accent said, 'Stop a moment; I wish to have a word with you. I am your friend.' I stopped and looked him full in the face, and he said, 'I saw you some days since in the slave-market, and I intended to have purchased you to save you from the condition of a slave. I called on Monday, but you had been sold and had left the market. I inquired and learned who the purchaser was, and that you had to go to Mobile, so I resolved to follow you. If you are willing, I will try and buy you from your present owner, and you shall be free.' Although this was said in an honest and off-hand manner, I could not believe the man to be sincere in what he said. 'Why should you wish to set *me* free?' I asked. 'I had an only sister,' he replied, 'who died three years ago in France, and you are so much like her, that had I not known of her death, I would most certainly have taken you for her.' 'However much I may resemble your sister, you are aware that I am not her, and why take so much interest in one whom you never saw before?' 'The love,' said he, 'which I had for my sister is transferred to you.' I had all along suspected that the man was a knave, and this profession of love confirmed me in my former belief, and I turned away and left him.

"The next day, while standing in the cabin and looking through the window, the French gentleman (for such he was) came to the window while walking on the guards, and again commenced as on the previous evening. He took from his pocket a bit of paper and put into my hand, and at the same time saying, 'Take this, it may some day be of service to you, remember it is from a friend,' and left me instantly. I unfolded the paper, and found it to be a 100 dols. bank note, on the United States Branch Bank, at Philadelphia. My first impulse was to give it to my mistress, but upon a second thought, I resolved to seek an opportunity, and to return the hundred dollars to the stranger. Therefore, I looked for him, but in vain; and had almost given up the idea of seeing him again, when he passed me on the guards of the boat and walked towards the stem of the vessel. It being now dark, I approached him and offered the money to him. He declined, saying at the same time, 'I gave it to you--keep it.' 'I do not want it,' I said. 'Now,' said he, 'you had better give your consent for me to purchase you, and you shall go with me to France.' 'But you cannot buy me now,' I replied, 'for my master is in New Orleans, and he purchased me not to sell, but to retain in his own family.' 'Would you rather remain with your present mistress, than be free?' 'No,' said I. 'Then fly with me to-night; we shall be in Mobile in two hours from this, and, when the passengers are going on shore, you can take my arm, and you can escape unobserved. The trader who brought you to New Orleans exhibited to me a certificate of your good character, and one from the Minister of the Church to which you were attached in Virginia; and upon the faith of these assurances, and the love I bear you, I promise before high heaven that I will marry you as soon as it can be done.' This solemn promise, coupled with what had already transpired, gave me confidence in the man; and rash as the act may seem, I determined in an instant to go with him. My mistress had been put under the charge of the captain; and as it would be past ten o'clock when the steamer would land, she accepted an invitation of the captain to remain on board with several other ladies till morning. I dressed myself in my best clothes, and put a veil over my face, and was ready on the landing of the boat. Surrounded by a number of passengers, we descended the stage leading to the wharf and were soon lost in the crowd that thronged the quay. As we went on shore we encountered several persons announcing the names of hotels, the starting of boats for the interior, and vessels bound for Europe. Among these was the ship *Utica*, Captain Pell, bound for Havre. 'Now,' said Mr. Devenant, 'this is our chance.' The ship was to sail at 12 o'clock that night, at high tide; and following the men who were seeking passengers, we went immediately on board. Devenant told the Captain of the ship that I was his sister, and for such we passed during the voyage. At the hour of twelve the *Utica* set sail, and we were soon out at sea.

"The morning after we left Mobile, Devenant met me as I came from my state-room and embraced me for the first time. I loved him, but it was only that affection which we have for one who has done us a lasting favour: it was the love of gratitude rather than that of the heart. We were five weeks on the sea, and yet the passage did not seem long, for Devenant was so kind. On our arrival at Havre, we were married and came to Dunkirk, and I have resided here ever since."

At the close of this narrative, the clock struck ten, when the old man, who was accustomed to retire at an early hour, rose to take leave, saying at the same time, "I hope you will remain with us to-night." Mr. Green would fain have excused himself, on the ground that they would expect him and wait at the hotel, but a look from the lady told him to accept the invitation. The old man was the father of Mrs. Devenant's deceased husband, as you will no doubt long since have supposed. A fortnight from the day on which they met in the grave-yard, Mr. Green and Mrs. Devenant were joined in holy wedlock; so that George and Mary, who had loved each other so ardently in their younger days, were now husband and wife. Without becoming responsible for the truthfulness of the above narrative, I give it to you, reader, as it was told to me in January last, in France, by George Green himself.

A celebrated writer has justly said of woman: "A woman's whole life is a history of the affections. The heart is her world; it is there her ambition strives for empire; it is there her avarice seeks for hidden treasures. She sends forth her sympathies on adventure; she embarks her whole soul in the traffic of affection; and if shipwrecked, her case is hopeless--for it is a bankruptcy of the heart."

Mary had every reason to believe that she would never see George again; and although she confesses that the love she bore him was never transferred to her first husband, we can scarcely find fault with her for marrying Mr. Devenant. But the adherence of George Green to the resolution never to marry, unless to his Mary, is, indeed, a rare instance of the fidelity of man in the matter of love. We can but blush for our country's shame, when we recall to mind the fact, that while George and Mary Green, and numbers of other fugitives from American slavery, can receive protection from any of the Governments of Europe, they cannot return to their native land without becoming slaves.

FINIS.

www.bookjungle.com email: sales@bookjungle.com fax: 630-214-0564 mail: Book Jungle PO Box 2226 Champaign, IL 61825

The Codes Of Hammurabi And Moses
W. W. Davies

QTY

The discovery of the Hammurabi Code is one of the greatest achievements of archaeology, and is of paramount interest, not only to the student of the Bible, but also to all those interested in ancient history...

Religion   **ISBN:** *1-59462-338-4*   **Pages:** 132
MSRP $12.95

The Theory of Moral Sentiments
Adam Smith

QTY

This work from 1749. contains original theories of conscience amd moral judgment and it is the foundation for systemof morals.

Philosophy   **ISBN:** *1-59462-777-0*   **Pages:** 536
MSRP $19.95

Jessica's First Prayer
Hesba Stretton

QTY

In a screened and secluded corner of one of the many railway-bridges which span the streets of London there could be seen a few years ago, from five o'clock every morning until half past eight, a tidily set-out coffee-stall, consisting of a trestle and board, upon which stood two large tin cans, with a small fire of charcoal burning under each so as to keep the coffee boiling during the early hours of the morning when the work-people were thronging into the city on their way to their daily toil...

Childrens   **ISBN:** *1-59462-373-2*   **Pages:** 84
MSRP $9.95

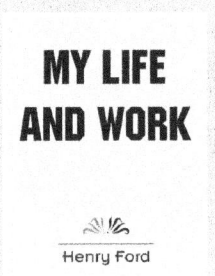

My Life and Work
Henry Ford

QTY

Henry Ford revolutionized the world with his implementation of mass production for the Model T automobile. Gain valuable business insight into his life and work with his own auto-biography... "We have only started on our development of our country we have not as yet, with all our talk of wonderful progress, done more than scratch the surface. The progress has been wonderful enough but..."

Biographies/   **ISBN:** *1-59462-198-5*   **Pages:** 300
MSRP $21.95

www.bookjungle.com *email: sales@bookjungle.com fax: 630-214-0564 mail: Book Jungle PO Box 2226 Champaign, IL 61825*

The Art of Cross-Examination
Francis Wellman

QTY

I presume it is the experience of every author, after his first book is published upon an important subject, to be almost overwhelmed with a wealth of ideas and illustrations which could readily have been included in his book, and which to his own mind, at least, seem to make a second edition inevitable. Such certainly was the case with me; and when the first edition had reached its sixth impression in five months, I rejoiced to learn that it seemed to my publishers that the book had met with a sufficiently favorable reception to justify a second and considerably enlarged edition. ..

Reference ISBN: *1-59462-647-2* Pages:412 MSRP *$19.95*

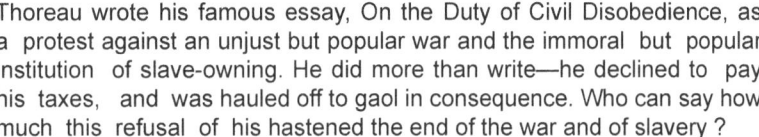

On the Duty of Civil Disobedience
Henry David Thoreau

QTY

Thoreau wrote his famous essay, On the Duty of Civil Disobedience, as a protest against an unjust but popular war and the immoral but popular institution of slave-owning. He did more than write—he declined to pay his taxes, and was hauled off to gaol in consequence. Who can say how much this refusal of his hastened the end of the war and of slavery ?

Law ISBN: *1-59462-747-9* Pages:48 MSRP *$7.45*

Dream Psychology Psychoanalysis for Beginners
Sigmund Freud

QTY

Sigmund Freud, born Sigismund Schlomo Freud (May 6, 1856 - September 23, 1939), was a Jewish-Austrian neurologist and psychiatrist who co-founded the psychoanalytic school of psychology. Freud is best known for his theories of the unconscious mind, especially involving the mechanism of repression; his redefinition of sexual desire as mobile and directed towards a wide variety of objects; and his therapeutic techniques, especially his understanding of transference in the therapeutic relationship and the presumed value of dreams as sources of insight into unconscious desires.

Psychology ISBN: *1-59462-905-6* Pages:196 MSRP *$15.45*

The Miracle of Right Thought
Orison Swett Marden

QTY

Believe with all of your heart that you will do what you were made to do. When the mind has once formed the habit of holding cheerful, happy, prosperous pictures, it will not be easy to form the opposite habit. It does not matter how improbable or how far away this realization may see, or how dark the prospects may be, if we visualize them as best we can, as vividly as possible, hold tenaciously to them and vigorously struggle to attain them, they will gradually become actualized, realized in the life. But a desire, a longing without endeavor, a yearning abandoned or held indifferently will vanish without realization.

Self Help ISBN: *1-59462-644-8* Pages:360 MSRP *$25.45*

www.bookjungle.com email: sales@bookjungle.com fax: 630-214-0564 mail: Book Jungle PO Box 2226 Champaign, IL 61825

QTY

☐ **The Rosicrucian Cosmo-Conception Mystic Christianity** *by Max Heindel* ISBN: *1-59462-188-8* **$38.95**
The Rosicrucian Cosmo-conception is not dogmatic, neither does it appeal to any other authority than the reason of the student. It is: not controversial, but is: sent forth in the, hope that it may help to clear... New Age/Religion Pages 646

☐ **Abandonment To Divine Providence** *by Jean-Pierre de Caussade* ISBN: *1-59462-228-0* **$25.95**
"The Rev. Jean Pierre de Caussade was one of the most remarkable spiritual writers of the Society of Jesus in France in the 18th Century. His death took place at Toulouse in 1751. His works have gone through many editions and have been republished... Inspirational/Religion Pages 400

☐ **Mental Chemistry** *by Charles Haanel* ISBN: *1-59462-192-6* **$23.95**
Mental Chemistry allows the change of material conditions by combining and appropriately utilizing the power of the mind. Much like applied chemistry creates something new and unique out of careful combinations of chemicals the mastery of mental chemistry... New Age Pages 354

☐ **The Letters of Robert Browning and Elizabeth Barret Barrett 1845-1846 vol II** ISBN: *1-59462-193-4* **$35.95**
by Robert Browning and Elizabeth Barrett Biographies Pages 596

☐ **Gleanings In Genesis (volume I)** *by Arthur W. Pink* ISBN: *1-59462-130-6* **$27.45**
Appropriately has Genesis been termed "the seed plot of the Bible" for in it we have, in germ form, almost all of the great doctrines which are afterwards fully developed in the books of Scripture which follow... Religion/Inspirational Pages 420

☐ **The Master Key** *by L. W. de Laurence* ISBN: *1-59462-001-6* **$30.95**
In no branch of human knowledge has there been a more lively increase of the spirit of research during the past few years than in the study of Psychology, Concentration and Mental Discipline. The requests for authentic lessons in Thought Control, Mental Discipline and... New Age/Business Pages 422

☐ **The Lesser Key Of Solomon Goetia** *by L. W. de Laurence* ISBN: *1-59462-092-X* **$9.95**
This translation of the first book of the "Lemegton" which is now for the first time made accessible to students of Talismanic Magic was done, after careful collation and edition, from numerous Ancient Manuscripts in Hebrew, Latin, and French... New Age/Occult Pages 92

☐ **Rubaiyat Of Omar Khayyam** *by Edward Fitzgerald* ISBN: *1-59462-332-5* **$13.95**
Edward Fitzgerald, whom the world has already learned, in spite of his own efforts to remain within the shadow of anonymity, to look upon as one of the rarest poets of the century, was born at Bredfield, in Suffolk, on the 31st of March, 1809. He was the third son of John Purcell... Music Pages 172

☐ **Ancient Law** *by Henry Maine* ISBN: *1-59462-128-4* **$29.95**
The chief object of the following pages is to indicate some of the earliest ideas of mankind, as they are reflected in Ancient Law, and to point out the relation of those ideas to modern thought. Religiom/History Pages 452

☐ **Far-Away Stories** *by William J. Locke* ISBN: *1-59462-129-2* **$19.45**
"Good wine needs no bush, but a collection of mixed vintages does. And this book is just such a collection. Some of the stories I do not want to remain buried for ever in the museum files of dead magazine-numbers an author's not unpardonable vanity..." Fiction Pages 272

☐ **Life of David Crockett** *by David Crockett* ISBN: *1-59462-250-7* **$27.45**
"Colonel David Crockett was one of the most remarkable men of the times in which he lived. Born in humble life, but gifted with a strong will, an indomitable courage, and unremitting perseverance... Biographies/New Age Pages 424

☐ **Lip-Reading** *by Edward Nitchie* ISBN: *1-59462-206-X* **$25.95**
Edward B. Nitchie, founder of the New York School for the Hard of Hearing, now the Nitchie School of Lip-Reading, Inc, wrote "LIP-READING Principles and Practice". The development and perfecting of this meritorious work on lip-reading was an undertaking... How-to Pages 400

☐ **A Handbook of Suggestive Therapeutics, Applied Hypnotism, Psychic Science** ISBN: *1-59462-214-0* **$24.95**
by Henry Munro Health/New Age/Health/Self-help Pages 376

☐ **A Doll's House: and Two Other Plays** *by Henrik Ibsen* ISBN: *1-59462-112-8* **$19.95**
Henrik Ibsen created this classic when in revolutionary 1848 Rome. Introducing some striking concepts in playwriting for the realist genre, this play has been studied the world over. Fiction/Classics/Plays 308

☐ **The Light of Asia** *by sir Edwin Arnold* ISBN: *1-59462-204-3* **$13.95**
In this poetic masterpiece, Edwin Arnold describes the life and teachings of Buddha. The man who was to become known as Buddha to the world was born as Prince Gautama of India but he rejected the worldly riches and abandoned the reigns of power when... Religion/History/Biographies Pages 170

☐ **The Complete Works of Guy de Maupassant** *by Guy de Maupassant* ISBN: *1-59462-157-8* **$16.95**
"For days and days, nights and nights, I had dreamed of that first kiss which was to consecrate our engagement, and I knew not on what spot I should put my lips..." Fiction/Classics Pages 240

☐ **The Art of Cross-Examination** *by Francis L. Wellman* ISBN: *1-59462-309-0* **$26.95**
Written by a renowned trial lawyer, Wellman imparts his experience and uses case studies to explain how to use psychology to extract desired information through questioning. How-to/Science/Reference Pages 408

☐ **Answered or Unanswered?** *by Louisa Vaughan* ISBN: *1-59462-248-5* **$10.95**
Miracles of Faith in China Religion Pages 112

☐ **The Edinburgh Lectures on Mental Science (1909)** *by Thomas* ISBN: *1-59462-008-3* **$11.95**
This book contains the substance of a course of lectures recently given by the writer in the Queen Street Hall, Edinburgh. Its purpose is to indicate the Natural Principles governing the relation between Mental Action and Material Conditions... New Age/Psychology Pages 148

☐ **Ayesha** *by H. Rider Haggard* ISBN: *1-59462-301-5* **$24.95**
Verily and indeed it is the unexpected that happens! Probably if there was one person upon the earth from whom the Editor of this, and of a certain previous history, did not expect to hear again... Classics Pages 380

☐ **Ayala's Angel** *by Anthony Trollope* ISBN: *1-59462-352-X* **$29.95**
The two girls were both pretty, but Lucy who was twenty-one who supposed to be simple and comparatively unattractive, whereas Ayala was credited, as her Bombwhat romantic name might show, with poetic charm and a taste for romance. Ayala when her father died was nineteen... Fiction Pages 484

☐ **The American Commonwealth** *by James Bryce* ISBN: *1-59462-286-8* **$34.45**
An interpretation of American democratic political theory. It examines political mechanics and society from the perspective of Scotsman James Bryce Politics Pages 572

☐ **Stories of the Pilgrims** *by Margaret P. Pumphrey* ISBN: *1-59462-116-0* **$17.95**
This book explores pilgrims religious oppression in England as well as their escape to Holland and eventual crossing to America on the Mayflower, and their early days in New England... History Pages 268

www.bookjungle.com email: sales@bookjungle.com fax: 630-214-0564 mail: Book Jungle PO Box 2226 Champaign, IL 61825

QTY

The Fasting Cure by *Sinclair Upton* ISBN: *1-59462-222-1* **$13.95**
In the Cosmopolitan Magazine for May, 1910, and in the Contemporary Review (London) for April, 1910, I published an article dealing with my experiences in fasting. I have written a great many magazine articles, but never one which attracted so much attention... New Age/Self Help/Health Pages 164

Hebrew Astrology by *Sepharial* ISBN: *1-59462-308-2* **$13.45**
In these days of advanced thinking it is a matter of common observation that we have left many of the old landmarks behind and that we are now pressing forward to greater heights and to a wider horizon than that which represented the mind-content of our progenitors... Astrology Pages 144

Thought Vibration or The Law of Attraction in the Thought World ISBN: *1-59462-127-6* **$12.95**
by *William Walker Atkinson* Psychology/Religion Pages 144

Optimism by *Helen Keller* ISBN: *1-59462-108-X* **$15.95**
Helen Keller was blind, deaf, and mute since 19 months old, yet famously learned how to overcome these handicaps, communicate with the world, and spread her lectures promoting optimism. An inspiring read for everyone... Biographies/Inspirational Pages 84

Sara Crewe by *Frances Burnett* ISBN: *1-59462-360-0* **$9.45**
In the first place, Miss Minchin lived in London. Her home was a large, dull, tall one, in a large, dull square, where all the houses were alike, and all the sparrows were alike, and where all the door-knockers made the same heavy sound... Childrens/Classic Pages 88

The Autobiography of Benjamin Franklin by *Benjamin Franklin* ISBN: *1-59462-135-7* **$24.95**
The Autobiography of Benjamin Franklin has probably been more extensively read than any other American historical work, and no other book of its kind has had such ups and downs of fortune. Franklin lived for many years in England, where he was agent... Biographies/History Pages 332

Name	
Email	
Telephone	
Address	
City, State ZIP	

☐ Credit Card   ☐ Check / Money Order

Credit Card Number	
Expiration Date	
Signature	

Please Mail to: Book Jungle
                  PO Box 2226
                  Champaign, IL 61825
or Fax to: 630-214-0564

ORDERING INFORMATION

web: *www.bookjungle.com*
email: *sales@bookjungle.com*
fax: *630-214-0564*
mail: *Book Jungle PO Box 2226 Champaign, IL 61825*
or PayPal *to sales@bookjungle.com*

Please contact us for bulk discounts

DIRECT-ORDER TERMS

**20% Discount if You Order
Two or More Books**
Free Domestic Shipping!
Accepted: Master Card, Visa,
Discover, American Express

www.ingramcontent.com/pod-product-compliance
Lightning Source LLC
Chambersburg PA
CBHW081225170426
43198CB00017B/2712